PROBLEMS IN EUROPEAN CIVILIZATION

UNDER THE EDITORIAL DIRECTION OF

Ralph W. Greenlaw

Other volumes in preparation

THE PIRENNE THESIS

Analysis, Criticism, and Revision

PROBLEMS IN EUROPEAN CIVILIZATION

THE
PIRENNE THESIS

*Analysis, Criticism,
and Revision*

EDITED WITH AN INTRODUCTION BY

Alfred F. Havighurst, AMHERST COLLEGE

D. C. HEATH AND COMPANY · BOSTON

Library of Congress Catalog Card Number: 58-12572

Copyright © 1958 by D. C. Heath and Company

PRINTED IN THE UNITED STATES OF AMERICA

Table of Contents

Introduction

"**D**URING the past generation a substantial literature has accumulated round one of the central problems of European history — the transition from the ancient world to medieval civilization." These words, the introductory sentence of one of the selections in this problem, were written twenty years ago, but the re-examination of the early Middle Ages, which they suggest, has continued.

The older view gave isolated and perfunctory treatment to Byzantium and to Islam and then turned wholeheartedly to the West: the Merovingians and Clovis, Charlemagne and the Carolingians, then the stem duchies in Germany and the Capetians in France, and the rest. *The Cambridge Medieval History* (8 v., 1911–1936), which brought together the scholarship of distinguished medievalists in many lands, did recognize the importance of Eastern Europe but still treated the Byzantine and Arab worlds quite apart from the West, and the emphasis throughout remained political and religious. Moreover, its character was encyclopedic with no interpretation integrating the enterprise as a whole. The abridged version (1952) was out of date at publication and it was then observed that the appearance of this *Shorter Cambridge Medieval History* probably marked the end of medieval history written as past politics organized around dynastic periods. For, under quite different controlling assumptions, the story of the early Middle Ages had long since been in the process of revision and by many of the very historians who had contributed to the conventional framework of the Cambridge history. As new questions were asked the

materials of the past returned to life, yielding greater knowledge and leading to new understanding.

To force re-examination of established ways of historical thinking requires powerful and original minds, and for the study of the Middle Ages there have been many such in the twentieth century: Ch. Diehl (French), Norman H. Baynes (British), A. A. Vasiliev (Russian and American), among Byzantine scholars; Philip Hitti (Lebanese and American) and E. Lévy-Provençal (French) on the Arabs and Islam; Alfons Dopsch, brilliant medievalist of Austria whose views made him a center of controversy; Marc Bloch, a hero of the French Resistance in World War II, who was a pioneer in French rural history; and so on. But if there was any one individual who in particular "upset the tranquility of the historian's world" and with whose name is associated special prestige, it was Henri Pirenne (1862–1935), celebrated national historian of Belgium and long associated with the university of Ghent. One encounters him wherever one turns in the historical writing of the past thirty years on the early Middle Ages.

Put in the most general terms the question which Pirenne faced, and which as a consequence of his writing the whole of medieval scholarship has confronted since, is that of the relation of Roman Antiquity to the medieval world of the First Europe. Some historians at least had been aware of what they were doing when they divided the story of western civilization into the Ancient World, the Middle Ages, and Modern Times. They realized of course that such artificial periodization denied the essential continuity of human experience. And it was well known that the very idea of the Middle Ages was the historical creation of another "period," that of the Renaissance, when humanist writers, at pains to identify their era with Antiquity, attributed a uniqueness to the centuries between. Yet repetition tends to influence thought. It came to be taken for granted that the "Ancient World" and the "Middle Ages" were easily distinguished the one from the other, and that a distinct break came in the fifth century with the disappearance of the "Roman" emperors in the West, the appearance of Germanic "barbarian" kingdoms, and the triumph of Christianity. These developments, with a slight accommodation, could be treated as simultaneous and dramatized in a comparatively brief span of years, and were considered sufficient to set off one "period" of the past from another. Such became the textbook point of view and, with some qualifications, a controlling assumption of scholars as well.

A quite radically different concept came out of the investigations of Pirenne. He concluded that the Roman world — economically, culturally, and even, in essence, politically — continued in all important particulars through the centuries of the German invasions. It was rather the impact of Islam in the seventh and eighth centuries which, by destroying the unity of the Mediterranean, ended the Roman world and led to a strikingly different civilization in the Carolingian era. "Without Islam the Frankish Empire would probably never have existed and Charlemagne, without Mohammet, would be inconceivable," he wrote in a famous sentence.

His countrymen tell us that this idea appeared in his lectures at Ghent as early as 1910. It was first given published form in articles in the *Revue belge de Philologie et d'Histoire,* in 1922. Pirenne popularized his concept the same year in a series of lectures delivered in American universities and published as *Medieval Cities,* in 1925. At the Sixth International Congress of Historical Sciences at Oslo in 1928, Pirenne read a paper on "L'expansion d'Islam et le commencement du moyen âge." A prolonged and animated discussion ensued — French, German, Polish, Italian, Dutch, and Hungarian scholars participating. Pirenne's views were amplified and documented in *Mahomet et Charlemagne,* finished in manuscript form only a few months before his death in 1935 and, unfortunately, never subject to a final revision by him. This work, published in 1937 and translated into English in 1939, brings together all of Pirenne's research on this theme. But *Medieval Cities* had long since given wide circulation to the "Pirenne Thesis." "No volume of similar size," wrote Professor Gray C. Boyce in 1941, "has so affected medieval historical scholarship in many generations."[1]

For economic historians of western Europe, Pirenne's views have had perhaps special significance. But the impact has been almost as great on Byzantine studies (for Pirenne lengthened the essential unity of the Roman Mediterranean world), upon historians of Germany (for Pirenne rather minimized the Germanic contribution to European development), upon historians of Islam whose story now assumed greater significance, and upon philosophers of history, such as Toynbee, especially concerned with theories of change.

The issues raised by Pirenne may be summarized as follows:

1. What developments distinguish Antiquity from the Middle Ages? When do we properly cease to speak of the Roman world and begin to think in terms of the First Europe?

2. What was the impact of Islam and the Arabs upon the West, and what that of the Germans?

3. What is the relation between the Merovingian era (roughly 5th to 8th centuries) and the Carolingian era (the 8th and 9th centuries)? Do they present essential continuity or are they in sharp contrast?

[1] *Byzantion,* XV, 460, n. 25.

4. What can historians say about trade and industry in the West, 400–1000?

It is to Pirenne's conclusions on these matters, to the controversy which his views precipitated and to the new vitality of early medieval studies to which they so powerfully contributed that the attention of the student is directed in this problem.

Our selections begin with brief introductory statements, in fresh and vigorous form, calculated to free the reader from any necessary adherence to conventional attitudes toward the period under consideration. One is from "The Formation of the First Europe," the opening chapter of a stimulating treatment by C. Delisle Burns in his *The First Europe* (1947). The other is an evaluation of the words "decay" and "decline" when used with reference to the Roman Empire, from an article by M. Rostovtzeff, one of the most important of Roman historians of the twentieth century.

Pirenne's own exposition is best studied, initially, in the popular and attractive *Medieval Cities.* This is the book which for well over a generation has made Pirenne's name familiar to undergraduate students of medieval history. Then from the more technical and more complete *Mohammed and Charlemagne,* we have his conclusions, in summary form, on the significance of the German invasions of Rome, a brief statement of the nature of the Islamic invasion of the Mediterranean and the West, and then a more elaborate examination of "Political Organization" and "Intellectual Civilization" in the Merovingian and Carolingian periods.

The remaining selections — consisting of discussion and criticism of the "Pirenne Thesis" — are chosen from a large body of commentary available. Some noted names are included, and from various national backgrounds. A French historian, J. Lestocquoy of Arras, examines the economy of the tenth century to determine if it will support Pirenne. From Professor Norman H. Baynes, an eminent British scholar in Byzantine studies, and from one of his associates, H. St. L. B. Moss, we have forthright criticism. An American scholar now at Yale, Professor Robert S. Lopez, who has undertaken research in one of the most difficult of fields — medieval economic history — makes a thorough analysis of the evidence. One of these extracts is from a paper read at the Tenth International Congress of Historical Sciences convening in Rome in 1955.

The writings of Pirenne have done much to stimulate research in directions quite different from those of his own investigations. Early medieval currencies, for example, is now a very active field of investigation. And consideration of the shift of civilization from the Mediterranean to northern Europe led Lynn White, Jr. to examine technological development. His article, "Technology and Invention in the Middle Ages," illustrates the extent to which Pirenne helped rescue historical scholarship from rather narrow and parochial concerns. From Daniel C. Dennett, Jr. we have an analysis of "Pirenne and Muhammad," by a specialist in Islamic history. And finally from a Danish scholar, Anne Riising, we have in her article, "The Fate of Henri Pirenne's Theses," an up-to-date consideration of the whole problem in the light of historical commentary of the past twenty-five years.

All together, these extracts present in sufficient detail for fairly close study the essentials of the "Pirenne Thesis." They also provide evidence and ideas against which to test its validity. Where does the matter now stand? Rather clearly Pirenne has left a permanent imprint upon medieval studies. Nearly every historian thinks differently because of him. And his central contribution, it would be generally agreed, has been this: to emancipate medieval historians in western Europe and in the United States from historical interests too exclusively political, legal, and religious in nature; to gain recognition of the importance of Islam and of the role of Byzantium in the story of western civilization; and to make historians more aware of the limits of understanding and the errors in interpretation which follow from easy periodization of European history. "Nothing is better proof of Pirenne's brilliant eloquence," writes Anne Riising, "than the fact that he has been able to impose his own formulation of the problems upon even his opponents."[2]

Yet, in particulars, research has generally refuted Pirenne. This in itself would not disturb him for he had no notion that he had entire historical truth. In 1932, as he finished the seventh and final volume of his great *Histoire de Belgique*, he insisted upon the value of works of historical synthesis which would suggest fresh hypotheses, establish new connections and pose different problems. At the same time he frankly admitted that any synthesis was necessarily provisional. "The materials [of history] can

never all be collected, for they can never be known. Problems cannot all be solved, for, as they are solved, new aspects are perpetually revealed. The historian opens the way; he does not close it."[3]

[NOTE : The statements in the *Conflict of Opinion* on page xv are from the following sources: Charles Oman, *The Dark Ages, 476–918* (1898), pp. 3, 5; Michael Postan, in *Cambridge Economic History of Europe*, vol. II (1952), p. 157; R. S. Lopez, *Relazioni del X Congresso Internazionale di Scienze Storiche*, vol. III, p. 129; Henri Pirenne, *Mohammed and Charlemagne*, p. 284, and *Medieval Cities*, p. 27; J. Lestocquoy, "The Tenth Century," *Economic History Review*, vol. XVII (1947), p. 1; Alfons Dopsch, quoted by H. St. L. B. Moss, *Economic History Review*, vol. VII (1936–1937), p. 214; R. S. Lopez, *Relazioni del X Congresso Internazionale di Scienze Storiche*, vol. III, p. 130; Norman H. Baynes, *Byzantine Studies and other Essays* (1955), pp. 315, 316; Lynn White, Jr., "Technology and Invention in the Middle Ages," *Speculum*, vol. XV (1940), pp. 152–153; Daniel C. Dennett, Jr., "Pirenne and Muhammad," *Speculum*, vol. XXIII (April 1948), pp. 168, 189–190.]

---

2 "The Fate of Henri Pirenne's Theses," *Classica et Mediaevalia*, XIII (1952), p. 130.

3 As paraphrased by F. M. Powicke, *Modern Historians and the Study of History* (London, 1955), p. 104.

CHRONOLOGICAL TABLE

Roman Empire

A.D. 284–305   DIOCLETIAN, *Roman Emperor*
306–337   CONSTANTINE I (THE GREAT), *Roman Emperor*
330   *Byzantium rebuilt as Constantinople*
379–395   THEODOSIUS I (THE GREAT), *Roman Emperor*
395   *Permanent division of Empire, East and West*
474–491   ZENO, *East Roman Emperor*
527–565   JUSTINIAN, *East Roman Emperor*
610–641   HERACLIUS I, *East Roman Emperor*
717–741   LEO III (THE ISAURIAN), *East Roman Emperor*

Germania

ca. 370   *Pressure of Huns on Goths in Eastern Europe*
378   *Battle of Adrianople; Visigoths defeat Romans*
395   *Huns (ATTILA) on the Danube*
451   *Final Defeat of Huns at Châlons (Champagne)*
395–408   *Visigothic Revolt (ALARIC) against Eastern Empire*
410   *Visigothic "Sack of Rome"*
ca. 400–600   *Visigothic Kingdom in Southern Gaul and Spain*
     (Continues in Spain until 711)
ca. 420   *Beginnings of Anglo-Saxon Invasions of Britain*
ca. 400–430   *Franks, Burgundians, Vandals cross the Rhine into Gaul*
ca. 400–600   *Burgundian Kingdom in Rhone Valley*
     (Absorbed by Franks, end of 6th century)
ca. 429–534   *Vandal Kingdom in North Africa*
     (Reconquered by JUSTINIAN)
455   *Vandals (GAISERIC) plunder Rome*
ca. 400–751   *Merovingian Kingdom of the Franks in Gaul*
481–511   CLOVIS, *Merovingian King of the Franks*
538–594   GREGORY, *Bishop of Tours (History of the Franks)*
639–751   *Rois Fainéants, Merovingian Kingdom of Franks in Gaul*

Romania

476   *Deposition of* ROMULUS AUGUSTUS, *last Roman-born Emperor of West*
476–493   ODOACER, *King of the Romans*
489   THEODORIC *leads Ostrogoths from Eastern Empire into Italy*
493–526   THEODORIC, *Ostrogothic King of Italy (Ravenna)*
ca. 480–575   CASSIODORUS, *Roman statesman and scholar*
480–525   BOETHIUS, *Roman statesman and philosopher*
535–553   JUSTINIAN'S *Reconquest (under* BELISARIUS) *of Africa, Italy, Sicily, and portions of Spain*
539–751   *Byzantine Exarchy in Ravenna*
552   *First appearance of Lombards (federated with Eastern Empire against the Ostrogoths)*
568   *Lombards conquer Po Valley*

Christianity

313	*Edict of Milan, Toleration of Christianity*
325	*Council of Nicaea*
354–430	SAINT AUGUSTINE OF HIPPO
379	*Death of* ST. BASIL
440–461	LEO I (THE GREAT), *Bishop of Rome ("Pope")*
480–534	ST. BENEDICT
ca. 590	ST. COLUMBAN (IRISH) *comes to Gaul*
590–604	POPE GREGORY I (THE GREAT)
597	ST. AUGUSTINE (BENEDICTINE) *lands in Britain*
ca. 673–735	THE VENERABLE BEDE
ca. 675–754	ST. BONIFACE

Islam

ca. 570–632	MOHAMMED
632	*Beginning of Caliphate* (ABU BAKR)
634–644	OMAR CALIPH *and Conquest of Syria, Persia, and Egypt*
661–750	OMAYYAD *Caliphate at Damascus*
661–680	MUAWIYA, *first Omayyad Caliph*
685–705	ABDU-L-MALIK, *Caliph*
711	*Islam reaches Spain*
732	*Battle of Tours*
750–1258	ABBASID *Caliphate at Bagdad*
786–809	HARUN-AL-RASCHID, *Caliph at Bagdad*

Carolingian Frankish Kingdom

687–714	PEPIN OF HERISTAL, *Mayor of the Palace*
714–741	CHARLES MARTEL, *Mayor of the Palace*
741–768	PEPIN THE SHORT, *Mayor of the Palace and (751) King of the Franks*
751	*Lombards take Ravenna*
768–814	CHARLEMAGNE, *King of the Franks, King of the Lombards, Emperor of the Romans*
782	ALCUIN OF YORK *comes to Palace School at Aachen*
800	*Coronation of* CHARLEMAGNE *as Emperor*
814–840	LOUIS THE PIOUS, *Emperor*
843	*Peace of Verdun, beginning of breakup of Carolingian Empire*

1. How was the world of antiquity which we call Roman transformed into the medieval society which we call European? From the days of Edward Gibbon to the early twentieth century, this question gave historians little trouble.

> If we must select any year as the dividing line between ancient history and the Middle Ages, it is impossible to choose a better date than 476 [the year in which the last Roman emperor, Romulus Augustus, was deposed by the German Odoacer]. . . . It is . . . in every way correct, as well as convenient to style him [Odoacer] as the first German king of Italy and to treat his reign as the commencement of a new era.
>
> — CHARLES OMAN

With this conclusion, economic development seemed to provide no difficulty.

> Without careful examination, historians could take it more or less for granted that the irruption of the barbarians meant a complete break with the economic civilization of the Roman Empire.
>
> — MICHAEL POSTAN

2. However, twentieth century historians have submitted the role of the Germans and the whole story of the transition to medieval society to reappraisal.

> Virtually nobody believes any more that the barbarian invasions of the fifth century marked a sharp turn in economic history, although most historians will admit that the meeting of German immaturity with Roman decrepitude accelerated the process of disintegration whose first symptoms can be traced as far back as the age of the Antonines.
>
> — R. S. LOPEZ

3. A brilliant contribution was made by Henri Pirenne, who put forth the view that the Moslems, not the Germans, destroyed the Roman world.

> The Germanic invasions destroyed neither the Mediterranean unity of the ancient world, nor what may be regarded as the truly essential features of Roman culture. . . . The cause of the break with the tradition of antiquity was the rapid and unexpected advance of Islam.
> Without Islam, the Frankish Empire would probably never have existed and Charlemagne, without Mahomet, would be inconceivable.

4. In more general terms Pirenne opened up a much larger question. Cannot much of the complexity of the transition from the Roman World to the Medieval World be understood through an analysis of economic change? Hence, it was essential to establish the relationship between the well-known Carolingian period (broadly the eighth and ninth centuries) and that which came before and that which followed. This is in itself a matter of some controversy.

The view which is at present the most widely accepted is that of Henri Pirenne. According to him, medieval civilization began to take shape at the end of the tenth century after the Viking and the Hungarian invasions had ceased. The end of the ancient world had come much earlier [with] the triumph of Islam . . . and the Carolingian period was one of full decline.

— J. Lestocquoy

The Carolingian development is a link in the unbroken chain of living continuity which leads, without any cultural break, from the late antiquity to the German middle ages.

— Alfons Dopsch

5. However, the ideas of both Pirenne and Dopsch have been sharply questioned.

Henri Pirenne made the Arabs squarely and directly responsible for pulling an iron curtain which separated the Believers from the Infidels and left Europe an economic and cultural dead end. His superb pleading and his personal charm won many converts. Nevertheless, a large number of scholars . . . were not convinced. For the last twenty years nearly all that has been written on early medieval economic history has reflected the heat of the controversy on "les thèses d'Henri Pirenne."

— R. S. Lopez

It is misleading to state that for the Franks of the sixth century, the Mediterranean still remained "mare nostrum." . . . My own belief is that the unity of the Mediterranean world was broken by the pirate fleet of Vandal Carthage and that the shattered unity was never restored.

— Norman H. Baynes

Pirenne is only the most recent of many historians to speculate as to why the reign of Charlemagne witnessed the shift of the center of European civilization, the change of the focus of history, from the Mediterranean to the plains of Northern Europe. The findings of agricultural history, it seems, have never been applied to this central problem. . . . For obvious reasons of climate the agricultural revolution of the eighth century was confined to Northern Europe.

— Lynn White, Jr.

6. And in recent years, our increased knowledge suggests once again a fresh appraisal.

We must affirm that . . . [in no authoritative statements in Islam] is there any prohibition against trading with the Christians or unbelievers. . . . Islam was hostile to Christianity as a rival, not as a completely alien faith, and the Muslims were invariably more tolerant than the Christians.

The man — whether he be a Pirenne or a Dopsch — who attempts to understand and to interpret either the Merovingian or Carolingian period in terms *purely* of an economic interpretation of history will be certain to fail, for the simple reason that economic factors play a subsidiary role and present merely aspects in the great causative process.

— Daniel C. Dennett, Jr.

THE FIRST EUROPE

C. DELISLE BURNS

Cecil Delisle Burns (1879–1942) had a varied and interesting career as an official in the British Ministry of Reconstruction created during World War I, as a party official in the Joint Research Department of the British Labor Party and Trades Union Congress, as an officer in the Labor Office of the League of Nations, and as a lecturer in Ethics and Social Philosophy in the University of London. His interests, as a writer, were in a sense equally diverse, for he ranged over all periods of history. But his books had a common theme—that of the relation of force and moral authority during periods of social transition. It is this theme which dominates *The First Europe*, the book from which a brief selection follows.

THE FIRST Europe came into existence during the four hundred years from the beginning of the fifth century to the end of the eighth century of the Christian era. It included, geographically, the countries now known as France, England, Ireland and southern Scotland, western Germany, central and northern Italy and northern Spain. Its peoples spoke Germanic languages in the North and East, and variations of Latin in the South and West. They were socially united in a Christendom which excluded the older eastern forms of Christianity; but they were divided by local lordships. This First Europe was, indeed, dependent in its earlier years upon the older cultures of the Mediterranean, which had produced finally the Roman Empire; but it was a new type of civilization. Thus, the word Europe became, after the collapse of the Roman Empire in the West, more than a geographical expression; and it was used in the new sense for the first time in the ninth century, for example, by Nithard the ninth-century historian, when he wrote that

Charles the Great at his death "had left all Europe in the greatest happiness." Europe is thus distinguished, not only from other lands, but from the tradition of the Greek-speaking Churches and Empire, and from Islam. From that time Europe was "the West" — not merely a different place but a different spirit.

The Roman Empire had never been European or Western, in the modern sense of these words. It had always united the countries surrounding the eastern Mediterranean, from which it drew its chief wealth, with the less developed countries of the West, including northern Gaul and Britain. And when, at the beginning of the fourth century, first Diocletian and then Constantine removed the central administration from Rome eastwards, it had become obvious to Roman generals and lawyers, as well as to the adherents of Christianity, that the real centre of the Empire lay at the junction of Asia and Europe. The Roman Empire was based upon the control of the trade routes in the basin of the Mediterranean. It inherited the conquests of the

From C. Delisle Burns, *The First Europe: A Study of the Establishment of Medieval Christendom, A.D. 400–800* (London, 1947), pp. 23–36. By permission of George Allen & Unwin Ltd.

1

Greek successors of Alexander in Egypt, Syria and Asia Minor. And although it had also succeeded to the conquests of the Roman Republic in the West, these were of less importance, three centuries after Augustus, than the rich and populous cities of what is now called the "Near East."

The civilization of the First Europe was quite distinct from the Roman. It did not depend upon the Mediterranean. It was the creation of the Latin Churches, and not of any one military or civil power. Its intellectual centres were in northern France, the Rhine country, England and northern Italy. Its architecture and other plastic arts were original experiments to meet new needs. Its music came out of popular songs. Its organizations of a learned caste, the clergy, of monasteries and of the universities which were later established, were new social inventions. Thus, the First Europe of the so-called Middle Ages, was an original experiment in new ways of living and thinking. Medieval civilization was more primitive than the Roman in externals, because it lacked, for example, baths and roads; and in culture it was more primitive, because it lacked that natural intercourse between educated men and women, which existed in the Roman villas and city mansions. But in other aspects it was an advance upon Mediterranean civilization; for example, in its moral and religious ideals, in its community of feeling between the rich and the poor and in its widespread sense of social responsibility. If character and conduct in different ages are to be compared, St. Francis was not more civilized than Seneca, but he had wider and more subtle sympathies; and Abelard, Aquinas and Occam were better thinkers than Cicero and Pliny, although their observation and experience were more limited. The greater philosophers of ancient Athens cannot be supposed to add credit to the Roman Empire, the culture and social organization of which retained few traces of their teaching in the fifth century of the Christian era. To avoid misunderstanding, therefore, it should be clearly stated that

medieval civilization is regarded here as only a first stage in the development of a pattern of culture, whose later forms were the second Europe of the sixteenth to nineteenth centuries, and the third Europe now being established. To compare the Roman system at its best under the Antonines, or in its later years under Constantine or Theodosius the Great, with the First Europe in the days of Charles the Great, is like comparing a great river, losing itself in the sands at the end of its course, with a mountain torrent from which a still greater stream arises. Or again, to change the metaphor, the early history of the First Europe treats of the roots of that great tree which has now expanded into modern science, modern music and arts, and modern skill in government. But the roots of that tree, if exposed to the light of history, may not appear so attractive as the latest faded flowers of Greek and Roman culture.

Although medieval civilization, throughout its whole course until the Renaissance, and certainly in its first years, was more primitive than the Roman, its roots struck far deeper among all classes of the community; and it contained forces much more powerful than the Roman Empire had ever included. The doctrine and practice of the Christian Churches, based upon the belief that each human being had an immortal soul to be saved, and that all were in some sense equal as Christians — this was one of the most important influences in the formation of what is now known as democracy. Democracy as an ideal means a social system of liberty, equality and fraternity for all men, and not a system in which a few share freedom among themselves in order the better to control the rest. And democracy as a system of government, by which the ideal may be approached, means at least some control by the "plain people" over their rulers and agents and some right of public discussion concerning public policy. But even in this sense, the sources of some elements in the democratic tradition of today are to be found in the election of bishops in the earliest Christian Churches and in the meeting of bishops as representatives in Synods, rather than in ancient Athens or Rome.

The word "democracy" in Greek did not refer to slaves and women as members of the political community, although, as in the case of cattle, their owners and masters might care for them. On the other hand, the Athenians developed and the Roman Republic preserved the power to criticize and remove public authorities and the free discussion of public policy by all citizens. But neither criticism nor discussion survived in the Christian Churches; and the democracy of early Christianity had passed, before the fifth century, into a form of despotism under the control of the bishops and clergy. The democratic tendency of Christianity in medieval Europe survived only in the sacraments and ceremonies, which were equally shared by all, and in early Christian documents which served at times to support protests against despotism, political or clerical. Nevertheless, democracy in the modern sense of that word, did in fact arise within the Christian tradition and not elsewhere. Medieval civilization was also the source of the great European literatures and of modern European music and plastic arts. Even modern experimental science can be traced to the practices of magic, both sacred and secular, in the Middle Ages. But in social institutions the early years of the First Europe were still more important for the future. At that time the system of nation-States had its origin in the barbarian kingdoms which replaced the Roman provinces in the West. The Roman organization of Christian communities spread from Italy and Gaul into England, Ireland and Germany. The great monastic system of the West was established; and pilgrimage connected the common people of all Europe. These are the roots of the First Europe. . . .

THE CONTRAST BETWEEN A.D. 400 AND A.D. 800

Of the most obvious institutions in A.D. 400 the Roman Empire is the best known. It was one system of government which included all the lands from northern Britain to the borders of Iraq, and from the Rhine and Danube to the Sahara. In A.D. 800, on the other hand, the same institution, still called the Roman Empire, included only part of the Balkan peninsula and of Turkey, within easy reach of its capital at Constantinople. But in western Europe separate kingdoms under Germanic chieftains were established in Gaul, then called western France, and Germany, then called eastern France, in Italy, in England and in northern Spain. The most striking feature of the change is the localization of government. Many different and independent centres of power and authority had taken the place of one; although all these countries were felt to be united against the outer world, as Latin Christendom. Africa north of the Sahara and southern Spain were ruled by Mohammedan Caliphs. In the East were unknown tribes; and in the West, the Ocean.

In A.D. 400 the Roman Emperors, who were Christian and Catholic, were legislating on doctrine and Church discipline, with the advice of bishops, who were themselves largely under the control of imperial officials. But by A.D. 800 there was an imperial Church, outside the surviving Roman Empire in the East, subject to the bishops of Rome, legislating for itself, and sometimes using the power of local kings for civil as well as ecclesiastical organization. A large part of western Europe was united again, but now by the organization of the Latin Churches, which had lost contact with the Christianity of the eastern Mediterranean. Less obvious, but more important than the great changes in political and ecclesiastical institutions, was the change in the system of production and distribution. In A.D. 400 the Roman Empire depended upon the organization of great cities — Rome, Constantinople, Alexandria, Carthage, Arles and the rest, whose populations obtained food and clothing from distant sources of supply. There was a trade in slaves, food-stuffs and raw materials throughout the Mediterranean basin, extending also to the Rhine country, northern Gaul and Britain. A cultured, city-bred, rich class provided administrators for a single system of economic customs and political laws. By A.D. 800 all this had disappeared from western Europe. The great Roman cities were in ruins; and their diminished populations continually suffered from plague, famine or the raids of armed gangs. Trade between the East and the West of the Mediterranean basin had almost come to an end. The slave-trade hardly existed; and neither ships nor road traffic were able to carry raw materials and foodstuffs for long distances. Distribution, therefore, had become local. It was organized by local landowners, controlling serfs tied to the soil, but possessed of customary rights. The ruling class, except for a few of the higher clergy, consisted of ignorant, illiterate, country-bred "sportsmen," whose chief enjoyment, when not killing or robbing their neighbours, was hunting game in the forests. In the four centuries that followed the fifth, a great process of de-urbanization was taking place. The population was more evenly spread over the whole area of north-western Europe. Thus, medieval Europe was embodied in the primitive castles and the abbeys and not, at any rate in its first phase, in the houses or churches of merchants and craftsmen in the towns.

Again, in A.D. 400 the centres of intellectual activity, of the arts and of trade, were the sea-ports of the Mediterranean basin — Constantinople, Alexandria, Carthage, Arles and Rome. By the ninth century the centres of activity in the First Europe lay in the North-West — Paris, Tours, Fulda, and, in later years, Antwerp and London. Thus the geographical setting for the new type of civilized life lay in countries on the border of the great ocean, which proved eventually to be, not the limit of the earth, but the pathway to a new world. Finally in A.D. 400 Christianity was a proselytizing religion, fighting long-established customs and beliefs of many different types; and Christianity itself, even

among the more simple-minded western races, was divided into different sects — Arians, Donatists, Priscillianists and others. It was organized in local congregations or Churches, each independent of the other, but connected by a common literature and ritual, and by the Councils of bishops. Later, in A.D. 800, in western Europe Christianity had become Christendom. Everyone was assumed to be Christian and Catholic. The Latin Churches of the West had coalesced into one imperial Church controlled by a separate caste of clergy, monks and nuns, most of them celibates, under the government, at least in theory, of the bishops of Rome.

ROMANS AND GERMANS

The contrast between A.D. 400 and A.D. 800 is startling. What is here attempted is to explain how and why the change occurred. In its earliest stages the change may be regarded as due to a conflict between a particular type of civilization and a particular type of barbarism. It is assumed in what follows that the "pattern of culture" called the Greek-Roman civilization, embodied in the late Roman Empire, was only one of many possible forms of civilized life. Not civilization in general, but only Roman civilization was in question in the fifth century, although most of the writers of that time thought of their own tradition as civilization itself. In the same way, some writers and speakers of to-day who lament the danger to "civilization," fail to perceive that an earlier pattern of culture may be replaced by a better. The Roman system was the last of the great predatory Empires based upon slavery; but it brought unity and extended culture throughout the countries in the basin of the Mediterranean. Its best products were regarded by eighteenth-century historians as standards for all civilized men; and they were therefore unable to understand or appreciate the new forms of civilization which took its place. But they were not wrong in supposing that any form of civilized life is better than any barbarism, although it is always difficult to distinguish the first signs of a new civilization from the barbarism by which it is surrounded.

This book is concerned with the transition from one type of civilization, the Roman, to another — the European. Any form of civilization is a complex of social relationships, more varied and more intricate than those of barbarism. Among civilized men and women opinions and tastes differ, and social customs are continually adjusted by individual experiment. Occupations are differentiated in what is called the division of labour, and the political and economic "interests" of the members of any community, and of different communities, are different and interdependent. In barbarism, on the other hand, all the members of the community are as far as possible alike in opinions, tastes, occupations and interests. Society is homogeneous. Established custom and belief control daily life and prevent variation. One man, or one caste of magicians or lords, provides the rules for thought and action. And therefore even in civilized communities the simplicity of barbarism has an attraction for minds weakened by personal distress or confused by social unrest, as it had for the Cynics in ancient Greece and the hermits of the third and fourth centuries of the Christian era.

Although civilization and barbarism are face to face, the chief purpose of our discussion is to show, not how an old civilization disappeared, but how a new civilization arose. Social relations change when a child becomes a man, when acquaintances become husband and wife, or when lovers use telephones instead of writing. When such changes occur, it is misleading to think of them as a decay or decline of an earlier system. It would be absurd to treat a change in social custom, such as the wearing of trousers instead of tunics in the fifth century, as a decay or decline of anything whatever. Biological metaphors applied to types of civilization or patterns of culture misrepresent the facts. Indeed, in times of social transition there is greater vitality among ordinary men and women

than at other times, precisely because the displacement of ancient customs compels them to think and act for themselves. Again, the transition from a long-established social system to the crude beginning of a new Order, must not be rendered in terms of good and bad. French is not bad Latin. But from the fifth to the ninth century, when the transition from Latin to French was taking place, the finer qualities of the new language were not so easily perceived, especially by the educated, as the mummified elegance of the Latin of the vanished past. As in the history of language, so in that of the plastic arts, the splendid temples of ancient Rome were more magnificent than the Christian basilicas of the fourth century and their mosaic decoration. But in the study of the transition to a new type of civilization it is necessary to foresee in the colours of the mosaics the future development of the decoration of the Christian Churches in the glass of the cathedrals of Chartres and of York. Thus, the transition from the Roman system of civilization must not be regarded primarily as the spread of barbarism.

On the other hand, the barbarism by which the Roman system was faced in the fifth century, was not barbarism in general, but a particular form of it. It was the barbarism of the Gothic and Germanic tribes introduced at first into the heart of the Roman world as its defenders. Historians of the nineteenth century, however, were as mistaken in their estimate of Germanic barbarism as their predecessors had been in their view of Roman culture. By the later historians, the Germanic barbarians were taken to be pure-souled, loyal and valiant supplanters of an effete social and political system. This astonishing mistake was, no doubt, partly due to a misunderstanding of the prejudices of the Christian Fathers, partly to the Romantic Movement, but chiefly to the uncontrolled imagination of sedentary scholars. As it is clear from contemporary records, the Germanic barbarians, with a few noble exceptions. were drunken, lecherous, cowardly and quite untrustworthy, even among those for whom they professed friendship. They did not indeed suffer from such vices of luxury as may be due to fine clothes, baths and good cooking. Simplicity has its attractions, even when, as Sidonius Apollinaris says, it stinks.[1] But the Vandals in Africa in the fifth century showed that the so-called virtues of barbarians were largely due to their ignorance of the more subtle tastes of civilized men. And it is an absurdity to treat Theodoric the Ostrogoth or Clovis the Frank as examples of nobility or valour. The first, with his own hand, killed his guest; the second split open the skull of a subordinate, when his back was turned. These men were savages. But the particular form of barbarism which can be contrasted with the Roman type of civilization in the fifth century, was certainly Germanic. A great German historian has said that "the process of barbarization of the Roman Empire was a process of Germanization."[2] The barbarism, therefore, with which this book is concerned, is not barbarism in general, but only one type of it.

In very general terms, the characteristics of Roman civilization and of Germanic barbarism may be described as follows. Under the Roman system the relations between men, women and children were complicated and various. A long-established system of slavery had been somewhat modified, under Stoic and Christian influence, to the advantage of the slaves. But the slave population was large; and even soldiers had slaves. Legal rights of ownership, marriage, inheritance and trade were clearly defined; and an official administration made them effectual. The mechanisms of production and transport were well developed. Public buildings and aqueducts still remain to prove the existence of applied sciences of which barbarians are ignorant. The minor arts of clothing and the preparation

of food were carried on in a characteristic form, as it is still evident in the Roman dress of the fifth century, which has served as a model for ecclesiastical costume and vestments surviving into modern times. The fine arts in the fifth century were superficial and derivative. Writers lived upon the pages of other writers, long since dead; and artists in the plastic arts spent their energies upon ornament rather than structure and function. But the fine arts had a recognized place in society.

Germanic barbarism, on the other hand, was the common characteristic of a number of disconnected small tribes, speaking dialects hardly yet developed into languages. Each of these tribes was as much, if not more, hostile to its neighbours than to the Roman Empire. The young men of these tribes, with some camp-followers, eagerly left the tribal settlements to seek booty or service in war under Roman commanders. They were simple folk, without any skill in agriculture, building or other useful arts, whose social relationships, as expressed in their legal customs, were troubled chiefly by personal violence, murder and stealing. That is to say, they were in that situation which sociologists describe as a transition from the pastoral to the agricultural stage of social development. In their entertainments and their religion, some customs and beliefs survived from a still earlier stage of social development — that of the hunters. Thus, even when the barbarians had entered into territories hitherto Roman, they preserved the pleasures of the chase and their belief in the magic of woods and sacred places. The members of a small barbarian community were, no doubt, more closely united in the simplicity of their minds, and in loyalty to their chieftains, than were the men and women of the more complex Roman city life. This may have been the basis of the idea of romantic historians that loyalty and honour were barbarian virtues. But any barbarian community faced two dangers. First, if it took service under one Roman general, it might be reduced to slavery by the victory of

---

[1] Felicemque libet vocare nasum, etc. (*Carm.* xxii. 13). "Happy the nose which cannot smell a barbarian." This was written about A.D. 455 in Gaul.

[2] Mommsen, *Romische Geschichte* (1885), Part v, bk. viii, ch. 4.

another; and, secondly, if it remained outside the Roman frontiers, it might suffer from the slave-raids which had been essential for many centuries before the fifth in order to supply the Roman world with cheap labour. No doubt, this is the basis for the idea that Germanic barbarians stood for "freedom." Tacitus wrote in the second century a brilliant political pamphlet on the "noble savage," the *Germania*. This attack upon the political opponents of Tacitus in Rome has been used, even in modern times, as evidence of the situation among the German tribes three hundred years after Tacitus wrote. But the Germanic barbarians were, like other barbarians, entangled in continually changing social situations, with their own defects and advantages. The same situations existed, in the main, among non-Germanic barbarians of the North, with whom the Roman populations came into contact — the Huns, the Avars, and the Slavs; but no Tacitus has made political capital out of these savages. Neither German nor other barbarians in the second or in the fifth century can be used by a modern historian as models of morality, with which to contrast the decadence of the Roman upper class. But the very simplicity of the barbarian mind in a barbarian society has its uses, if a new step is to be made in the history of civilized life. At least a futile culture will be brought down to common earth.

The barbarian warriors and the tribes from which they came, were not opposed to Roman civilization, and certainly did not mean to destroy it. Indeed, they asked nothing better than to be allowed to share in its products — food, wealth, security and more refined pleasures. Barbarian warriors sought pay or booty; and in the later fifth century discovered that they could obtain more wealth by settling among a civilized population than by looting and moving from place to place. There were barbarian settlements within the Roman frontiers, and thousands of Germanic slaves there, before there were barbarian invasions. But even the barbarians who invaded Italy and Gaul did not attempt to destroy the Roman social system or the Roman Empire which maintained it. They desired only to plunder a building which was already falling into ruins. And on the other hand, the policy of the later Roman Emperors was that called "appeasement" in modern times. For example, the Visigoths and Burgundians were granted leave to retain their conquests, in the hope that they would not take any more. The Vandals were invited into Africa by a Roman General. The Ostrogoths, under Theodoric, conquered Italy with the acquiescence and perhaps the approval of the Roman Emperor at Constantinople. It is probably true, as was supposed at the time, that the Lombards entered Italy at the request of a Roman Exarch. And after "appeasement" had allowed the establishment of barbarian kingdoms in Gaul, Spain, Africa and Italy, Justinian's attempt in the sixth century to adopt the opposite policy proved to be quite futile. It came too late to save the Roman provinces in the West.

From the point of view of the governing class in the Roman Empire, there was no hostility to the Germanic barbarians. The Emperors and the Roman generals desired to use them. They welcomed them as soldiers, and found them useful and also decorative as slaves. The imperial Authorities, in fear of civil war, had forbidden men of senatorial rank to join the army, and were not eager to recruit the legions from the city populations, which had various other duties to perform in industry and transport. In consequence the majority of the Romanized city and country population in western Europe was demilitarized; and the best recruits for the armed forces were found among the barbarian tribes. Thus, in the fifth century, the word "soldier" (miles) was equivalent in meaning to the word "barbarian" (barbarus). The situation thus created may be regarded as an attempt to civilize the barbarians, by using them for the only services for which they were competent within the Roman system. But to the minds of men of the fifth century, to civilize meant to Romanize; and the barbarians themselves accepted this idea. The result was obvious. While it became more doubtful in what institution or persons moral authority was to be found, clearly armed force, and the wealth and power which it could obtain, fell more completely into the hands of the barbarians as the years went by. The barbarians were not only soldiers of the line and cavalry, but generals and even Emperors. The Emperor Justin, the uncle of the great Justinian, could neither read nor write. Here again, then, it must be repeated that the problem was not that of civilization in general, but of the Roman form of it. A similar problem in the modern world exists in Africa. Europeans desire to civilize the Africans; and the Africans desire to be civilized. But because both assume that the only form of civilization in question is the European, Europeans attempt to Europeanize the Africans. Some Europeans believe that Africans can be used only as cheap labour, exactly as Romans of the fifth century be-

lieved that Germanic barbarians could be useful only as slaves or soldiers. And, on the other hand, some Africans, in their attempt to escape from the pastoral and agricultural stages of social development into what they believe to be civilization, have contrived to become Europeanized. The result is satisfactory neither to Africans nor Europeans. As in the fifth century in western Europe, a particular type of civilization has not proved flexible enough to meet new strains and pressures. The Roman crisis has come to an end; and that in modern Africa has hardly begun. But it is still possible that modern European civilization will be more successful than the Roman in adapting itself to new experiences and alien influences. From this point of view, the Middle Ages were centuries during which, after the failure to adjust the Roman system to the play of new forces, these forces built up a new kind of civilized life and culture in its first form. . . .

The Terms "DECAY" and "DECLINE AND FALL"

M. ROSTOVTSEFF

M. Rostovtseff (1870–1952) was already well known as a classicist at St. Petersburg in his native Russia before he came to the United States in 1920. He was professor of ancient history at Wisconsin until 1925 and subsequently professor of ancient history and archaeology at Yale until his retirement in 1944. The last few years he was also Director of Archaeological Studies and was in charge of the work at Dura near ancient Babylon. As a scholar and as a teacher he ranks among the most important ancient historians of the twentieth century. His honors were many, including the presidency of the American Historical Association in 1935. His greatest contribution was made as an economic historian of the ancient world; his most important works were *Social and Economic History of the Roman Empire* (1926) and *Social and Economic History of the Hellenistic World,* 3 vols. (1941). The extract below is from a scholarly article in which he discussed various economic explanations for the age-old question of the decline of Rome.

LET ME DEFINE briefly what I mean by the Gibbonian term "decay" or "decline and fall." We are learning gradually that the term "decay" can hardly be applied to what happened in the ancient world in the time of the late Roman Empire and the beginning of the so-called Middle Ages. Historians do not recognize that there was anything like "decay" of civilization in these periods. What happened was a slow and gradual change, a shifting of values in the consciousness of men. What seemed to be all-important to a Greek of the classical or Hellenistic period, or to an educated Roman of the time of the Republic and of the Early Empire, was no longer regarded as vital by the majority of men who lived in the late Roman Empire and the Early Middle Ages. They had their own notion of what was important, and most of what was essential in the classical period among the constituent parts of ancient civilization was discarded by them as futile and often detrimental. Since our point of view is more or less that of the classical peoples, we regard such an attitude of mind as a relapse into "barbarism," which in fact it is not.

Let me quote some striking examples. I am not referring to the gradual disintegration of the Roman Empire. Politically it might be called the "Fall" of the Roman Empire — that is, of that form of government which had for some centuries united almost the whole of the civilized world into one state. Whether the creation of the Roman Empire in itself was a blessing for the human race is a question under debate. Many prominent historians think that it was more or less of a calamity. It is still more problematic whether the disintegration of the Roman Empire was detrimental for the world or not. Without this disintegration we should not have, among other

From M. Rostovtseff, "The Decay of the Ancient World and Its Economic Explanations," *The Economic History Review,* II (January, 1930), 197–199. By permission of Mrs. Sophie Rostovtseff and *The Economic History Review.*

things, . . . the great national states of to-day (if not of to-morrow). From the point of view of "ancient" *civilization* the late Roman Empire was no doubt a period of great simplification — barbarization as we call it — or, better, a period of the reduction of ancient civilization to some essential elements which survived while the rest disappeared.

This process of disintegration and simplification is, however, only one aspect of the phenomenon we are dealing with. While the fabric of the ancient Roman Empire was disintegrating, the Christian Church, whose organization was more or less reproducing that of the State, was thriving and gaining in ecumenic powers. While philosophical thought and scientific endeavours of the Greek type were gradually dying out, theology took an unprecedented development and satisfied the needs of the majority of those who cared for intellectual life. And in the field of art there was, in this time of supposed decay, one triumph after another. We are gradually learning to appreciate the originality and force of the late Roman "pagan" art, and we have already learned to admire the early products of Christian art both in architecture and in sculpture and especially in painting (including the mosaics).

And, last but not least, while in the West the heirs of ancient cities gave birth to fresh and vigorous germs of a new civilization, both different and similar if compared with the old, in the East the same classical civilization in its modified Christian aspect was still alive and thriving, and in the long period of its life experienced many temporary declines and many brilliant revivals. Even in the West, not everything during the centuries after the great crisis of the third century was misery and ruin. The fourth century witnessed a strong revival both from the political and the economic point of view, and this revival was not of short duration.

Thus to apply to events in the ancient world in the centuries after Diocletian and Constantine the term "decay" or "decline" is unfair and misleading. If, however, in the formula "decay of ancient civilization" we lay stress on "ancient" and not on "civilization," the formula hits the point. No doubt "ancient" — that is, "Greco-Roman" — civilization, the civilization of the world of Greco-Roman cities, of the Greek "politai" and Roman "cives," was gradually simplified, barbarized, reduced to its elements, and the bearers of this civilization, the cities and their inhabitants, gradually disappeared or changed their aspect almost completely. . . .

From *MEDIEVAL CITIES*

HENRI PIRENNE

THE MEDITERRANEAN

THE ROMAN EMPIRE, at the end of the third century, had one outstanding general characteristic: it was an essentially Mediterranean commonwealth. Virtually all of its territory lay within the watershed of that great land-locked sea; the distant frontiers of the Rhine, the Danube, the Euphrates and the Sahara, may be regarded merely as an advanced circle of outer defenses protecting the approaches.

The Mediterranean was, without question, the bulwark of both its political and economic unity. Its very existence depended on mastery of the sea. Without that great trade route, neither the government, nor the defense, nor the administration of the *orbis romanus* would have been possible.

As the Empire grew old this fundamentally maritime character was, interestingly enough, not only preserved but was still more sharply defined. When the former inland capital, Rome, was abandoned, its place was taken by a city which not only served as a capital but which was at the same time an admirable seaport—Constantinople.

The Empire's cultural development, to be sure, had clearly passed its peak. Population decreased, the spirit of enterprise waned, barbarian hordes commenced to threaten the frontiers, and the increasing expenses of the government, fighting for its very life, brought in their train a fiscal system which more and more enslaved men to the State. Nevertheless this general deterioration does not seem to have appreciably affected the maritime commerce of the Mediterranean. It continued to be active and well sustained, in marked contrast with the growing apathy that characterized the inland provinces. Trade continued to keep the East and the West in close contact with each other. There was no interruption to the intimate commercial relations between those diverse climes bathed by one and the same sea. Both manufactured and natural products were still extensively dealt in: textiles from Constantinople, Edessa, Antioch, and Alexandria; wines, oils, and spices from Syria; papyrus from Egypt; wheat from Egypt, Africa, and Spain; and wines from Gaul and Italy. There was even a reform of the monetary system based on the gold *solidus,* which served materially to encourage commercial operations by giving them the benefit of an excellent currency, universally adopted as an instrument of exchange and as a means of quoting prices.

Of the two great regions of the Empire, the East and the West, the first far surpassed the second, both in superiority of civilization and in a much higher level of economic development. At the beginning of the fourth century there were no longer any really great cities save in the East. The center of the export trade was in Syria and in Asia Minor, and here also was concentrated, in particular, the textile industry

From Henri Pirenne, *Medieval Cities: Their Origins and the Revival of Trade* (Princeton, 1925), pp. 3–55. By permission of the Princeton University Press, and the Oxford University Press.

for which the whole Roman world was the market and for which Syrian ships were the carriers.

The commercial prominence of the Syrians is one of the most interesting facts in the history of the Lower Empire. It undoubtedly contributed largely to that progressive orientalization of society which was due eventually to end in Byzantinism. And this orientalization, of which the sea was the vehicle, is clear proof of the increasing importance which the Mediterranean acquired as the aging Empire grew weak, gave way in the North beneath the pressure of the barbarians, and contracted more and more about the shores of this inland sea.

The persistence of the Germanic tribes in striving, from the very beginning of the period of the invasions, to reach these same shores and to settle there is worth special notice. When, in the course of the fourth century, the frontiers gave way for the first time under their blows, they poured southward in a living flood. The Quadi and the Marcomanni invaded Italy; the Goths marched on the Bosporus; the Franks, the Suevi, and the Vandals, who by now had crossed the Rhine, pushed on unhesitatingly towards Aquitaine and Spain. They had no thought of merely colonizing the provinces they coveted. Their dream was rather to settle down, themselves, in those happy regions where the mildness of the climate and the fertility of the soil were matched by the charms and the wealth of civilization.

This initial attempt produced nothing more permanent than the devastation which it had caused. Rome was still strong enough to drive the invaders back beyond the Rhine and the Danube. For a century and a half she succeeded in restraining them, but at the cost of exhausting her armies and her finances.

More and more unequal became the balance of power. The incursions of the barbarians grew more relentless as their increasing numbers made the acquisition of new territory more imperative, while the decreasing population of the Empire made a successful resistance constantly less pos-

sible. Despite the extraordinary skill and determination with which the Empire sought to stave off disaster, the outcome was inevitable.

At the beginning of the fifth century, all was over. The whole West was invaded. Roman provinces were transformed into Germanic kingdoms. The Vandals were installed in Africa, the Visigoths in Aquitaine and in Spain, the Burgundians in the Valley of the Rhône, the Ostrogoths in Italy.

This nomenclature is significant. It includes only Mediterranean countries, and little more is needed to show that the objective of the conquerors, free at last to settle down where they pleased, was the sea — that sea which for so long a time the Romans had called, with as much affection as pride, *mare nostrum*. Towards the sea, as of one accord, they all turned their steps, impatient to settle along its shores and to enjoy its beauty.

If the Franks did not reach the Mediterranean at their first attempt, it is because, having come too late, they found the ground already occupied. But they too persisted in striving for a foothold there. One of Clovis's earliest ambitions was to conquer Provence, and only the intervention of Theodoric kept him from extending the frontiers of his kingdom as far as the Côte d'Azur. Yet this first lack of success was not due to discourage his successors. A quarter of a century later, in 536, the Franks made good use of Justinian's offensive against the Ostrogoths and wrung from their hard-pressed rivals the grant of the coveted territory. It is interesting to see how consistently the Merovingian dynasty tended, from that date on, to become in its turn a Mediterranean power.

Childebert and Clotaire, for example, ventured upon an expedition beyond the Pyrenees in 542, which, however, proved to be ill-starred. But it was Italy in particular that aroused the cupidity of the Frankish kings. They formed an alliance, first with the Byzantines and then with the Lombards, in the hope of setting foot south of the

Alps. Repeatedly thwarted, they persisted in fresh attempts. By 539, Theudebert had crossed the Alps, and the territories which he had occupied were reconquered by Narses in 553. Numerous efforts were made in 584–585 and from 588 to 590 to get possession anew.

The appearance of the Germanic tribes on the shore of the Mediterranean was by no means a critical point marking the advent of a new era in the history of Europe. Great as were the consequences which it entailed, it did not sweep the boards clean nor even break the tradition. The aim of the invaders was not to destroy the Roman Empire but to occupy and enjoy it. By and large, what they preserved far exceeded what they destroyed or what they brought that was new. It is true that the kingdoms they established on the soil of the Empire made an end of the latter in so far as being a *State* in Western Europe. From a political point of view the *orbis romanus*, now strictly localized in the East, lost that ecumenical character which had made its frontiers coincide with the frontiers of Christianity. The Empire, however, was far from becoming a stranger to the lost provinces. Its civilization there outlived its authority. By the Church, by language, by the superiority of its institutions and law, it prevailed over the conquerors. In the midst of the troubles, the insecurity, the misery and the anarchy which accompanied the invasions there was naturally a certain decline, but even in that decline there was preserved a physiognomy still distinctly Roman. The Germanic tribes were unable, and in fact did not want, to do without it. They barbarized it, but they did not consciously germanize it.

Nothing is better proof of this assertion than the persistence in the last days of the Empire — from the fifth to the eighth century — of that maritime character pointed out above. The importance of the Mediterranean did not grow less after the period of the invasions. The sea remained for the Germanic tribes what it had been before their arrival — the very center of Europe,

the *mare nostrum.* The sea had had such great importance in the political order that the deposing of the last Roman Emperor in the West (476) was not enough in itself to turn historical evolution from its time-honored direction. It continued, on the contrary, to develop in the same theater and under the same influences. No indication yet gave warning of the end of that commonwealth of civilization created by the Empire from the Pillars of Hercules to the Aegean Sea, from the coasts of Egypt and Africa to the shores of Gaul, Italy and Spain. In spite of the invasion of the barbarians the new world conserved, in all essential characteristics, the physiognomy of the old. To follow the course of events from Romulus Augustulus to Charlemagne it is necessary to keep the Mediterranean constantly in view.

All the great events in political history are unfolded on its shores. From 493 to 526 Italy, governed by Theodoric, maintained a hegemony over all the Germanic kingdoms, a hegemony through which the power of the Roman tradition was perpetuated and assured. After Theodoric, this power was still more clearly shown. Justinian failed by but little of restoring imperial unity (527–565). Africa, Spain, and Italy were reconquered. The Mediterranean became again a Roman lake. Byzantium, it is true, weakened by the immense effort she had just put forth, could neither finish nor even preserve intact the astonishing work which she had accomplished. The Lombards took Northern Italy away from her (568); the Visigoths freed themselves from her yoke. Nevertheless she did not abandon her ambitions. She retained, for a long time to come, Africa, Sicily, Southern Italy. Nor did she loose her grip on the West — thanks to the sea, the mastery of which her fleets so securely held that the fate of Europe rested at that moment, more than ever, on the waves of the Mediterranean.

What was true of the political situation held equally well for the cultural. It seems hardly necessary to recall that Boëthius (480–525) and Cassiodorus (477–c. 562) were Italians as were St. Benedict (480–534) and Gregory the Great (590–604), and that Isidorus of Seville (570–636) was a Spaniard. It was Italy that maintained the last schools at the same time that she was fostering the spread of monachism north of the Alps. It was in Italy, also, that what was left of the ancient culture flourished side by side with what was brought forth anew in the bosom of the Church. All the strength and vigor that the Church possessed was concentrated in the region of the Mediterranean. There alone she gave evidence of an organization and spirit capable of initiating great enterprises. An interesting example of this is the fact that Christianity was brought to the Anglo-Saxons (596) from the distant shores of Italy, not from the neighboring shores of Gaul. The mission of St. Augustine is therefore an illuminating sidelight on the historic influence retained by the Mediterranean. And it seems more significant still when we recall that the evangelization of Ireland was due to missionaries sent out from Marseilles, and that the apostles of Belgium, St. Amand (689–693) and St. Remade (c. 668), were Aquitanians.

A brief survey of the economic development of Europe will give the crowning touch to the substantiation of the theory which has here been put forward. That development is, obviously, a clear-cut, direct continuation of the economy of the Roman Empire. In it are rediscovered all the latter's principal traits and, above all, that Mediterranean character which here is unmistakable. To be sure, a general decline in social activity was apparent in this region as in all others. By the last days of the Empire there was a clearly marked decline which the catastrophe of the invasions naturally helped accentuate. But it would be a decided mistake to imagine that the arrival of the Germanic tribes had as a result the substitution of a purely agricultural economy and a general stagnation in trade for urban life and commercial activity.

The supposed dislike of the barbarians for towns is an admitted fable to which reality has given the lie. If, on the extreme frontiers of the Empire, certain towns were put to the torch, destroyed and pillaged, it is none the less true that the immense majority survived the invasions. A statistical survey of cities in existence at the present day in France, in Italy and even on the banks of the Rhine and the Danube, gives proof that, for the most part, these cities now stand on the sites where rose the Roman cities, and that their very names are often but a transformation of Roman names.

The Church had of course closely patterned the religious districts after the administrative districts of the Empire. As a general rule, each diocese corresponded to a *civitas*. Since the ecclesiastical organization suffered no change during the era of the Germanic invasions, the result was that in the new kingdoms founded by the conquerors it preserved intact this characteristic feature. In fact, from the beginning of the sixth century the word *civitas* took the special meaning of "episcopal city," the center of the diocese. In surviving the Empire on which it was based, the Church therefore contributed very largely to the safeguarding of the existence of the Roman cities.

But it must not be overlooked, on the other hand, that these cities in themselves long retained a considerable importance. Their municipal institutions did not suddenly disappear upon the arrival of the Germanic tribes. Not only in Italy, but also in Spain and even in Gaul, they kept their *decuriones* — a corps of magistrates provided with a judicial and administrative authority, the details of which are not clear but whose existence and Roman origin is a matter of record. There is to be noticed, moreover, the presence of the *defensor civitatis,* and the practice of inscribing notarized deeds in the *gesta municipalia.*

It is also well established that these cities were the centers of an economic activity which itself was a survival of the preceding civilization. Each city was the market for the surrounding countryside, the winter home of the great landed proprietors of the neighborhood and, if favorably situated, the center of a commerce the more highly developed in proportion to its nearness to the shores of the Mediterranean. A perusal of Gregory of Tours gives ample proof that in the Gaul of his time there was still a professional merchant class residing in the towns. He cites, in some thoroughly characteristic passages, those of Verdun, Paris, Orleans, Clermont-Ferrand, Marseilles, Nîmes, and Bordeaux, and the information which he supplies concerning them is all the more significant in that it is brought into his narrative only incidentally. Care should of course be taken not to exaggerate its value. An equally great fault would be to undervalue it. Certainly the economic order of Merovingian Gaul was founded on agriculture rather than on any other form of activity. More certainly still this had already been the case under the Roman Empire.

But this does not preclude the fact that inland traffic, the import and export of goods and merchandise, was carried on to a considerable extent. It was an important factor in the maintenance of society. An indirect proof of this is furnished by the institution of market-tolls. Thus were called the tolls set up by the Roman administration along the roads, in the ports, at bridges and fords, and elsewhere. The Frankish kings let them all stay in force and drew from them such copious revenues that the collectors of this class of taxes figured among their most useful functionaries.

The continued commercial activity after the disappearance of the Empire, and, likewise, the survival of the towns that were the centers thereof and the merchants who were its instruments, is explained by the continuation of Mediterranean trade. In all the chief characteristics it was the same, from the fifth to the eighth centuries, as it had been just after Constantine. If, as is probable, the decline was the more rapid after the Germanic invasions, it remains none the less true that there is presented a picture of uninterrupted intercourse between the Byzantine East and the West dominated by the barbarians. By means of the shipping which was carried on from the coasts of Spain and Gaul to those of Syria and Asia Minor, the basin of the Mediterranean did not cease, despite the political subdivisions which it had seen take place, to consolidate the economic unity which it had shaped for centuries under the imperial commonwealth. Because of this fact, the economic organization of the world lived on after the political transformation.

In lack of other proofs, the monetary system of the Frankish kings would alone establish this truth convincingly. This system, as is too well known to make necessary any lengthy consideration here, was purely Roman or, strictly speaking, Romano-Byzantine. This is shown by the coins that were minted: the *solidus*, the *triens*, and the *denarius* — that is to say, the *sou*, the *third-sou* and the *denier*. It is shown further by the metal which was employed: gold, used for the coinage of the *solidus* and the *triens*. It is also shown by the weight which was given to specie. It is shown, finally, by the effigies which were minted on the coins. In this connection it is worth noting that the mints continued for a long time, under the Merovingian kings, the custom of representing the bust of the Emperor on the coins and of showing on the reverse of the pieces the *Victoria Augusti* and that, carrying this imitation to the extreme, when the Byzantines substituted the cross for the symbol of that victory they did the same. Such extreme servility can be explained only by the continuing influence of the Empire. The obvious reason was the necessity of preserving, between the local currency and the imperial currency, a conformity which would be purposeless if the most intimate relations had not existed between Merovingian commerce and the general commerce of the Mediterranean. In other words, this commerce continued to be closely bound up with the commerce of the Byzantine Empire. Of such ties, moreover, there are abundant proofs and it will suffice to mention merely a few of the most significant.

It should be borne in mind, first of all,

that at the start of the eighth century
Marseilles was still the great port of Gaul.
The terms employed by Gregory of Tours,
in the numerous anecdotes in which he
happens to speak of that city, make it seem
a singularly animated economic center. A
very active shipping bound it to Constantinople, to Syria, Africa, Egypt, Spain and
Italy. The products of the East — papyrus,
spices, costly textiles, wine and oil — were
the basis of a regular import trade. Foreign
merchants, Jews and Syrians for the most
part, had their residence there, and their
nationality is itself an indication of the
close relations kept up by Marseilles with
Byzantium. Finally, the extraordinary
quantity of coins which were struck there
during the Merovingian era gives material
proof of the activity of its commerce. The
population of the city must have comprised,
aside from the merchants, a rather numerous class of artisans. In every respect it
seems, then, to have accurately preserved,
under the government of the Frankish
kings, the clearly municipal character of
Roman cities.

The economic development of Marseilles
naturally made itself felt in the hinterland
of the port. Under its attraction, all the
commerce of Gaul was oriented toward the
Mediterranean. The most important market-
tolls of the Frankish kingdom were situated
in the neighborhood of the town at Fos, at
Arles, at Toulon, at Sorgues, at Valence,
at Vienne, and at Avignon. Here is clear
proof that merchandise landed in the city
was expedited to the interior. By the course
of the Rhône and of the Saone, as well as
by the Roman roads, it reached the north
of the country. The charters are still in
existence by which the Abbey of Corbie
(Department of Pas-de-Calais) obtained
from the kings an exemption from tolls at
Fos on a number of commodities, among
which may be remarked a surprising variety
of spices of eastern origin, as well as papyrus. In these circumstances it does not seem
unwarranted to assume that the commercial
activity of the ports of Rouen and Nantes,
on the shores of the Atlantic Ocean, as well

as of Quentovic and Duurstede, on the
shores of the North Sea, was sustained by
the ramifications of the export traffic from
far-off Marseilles.

But it was in the south of the country
that this effect was the most appreciable.
All the largest cities of Merovingian Gaul
were still to be found, as in the days of the
Roman Empire, south of the Loire. The
details which Gregory of Tours supplies
concerning Clermont-Ferrand and Orleans
show that they had within their walls veritable colonies of Jews and Syrians, and if
it was so with those towns which there is
no reason for believing enjoyed a privileged
status, it must have been so also with the
much more important centers such as
Bordeaux or Lyons. It is an established
fact, moreover, that Lyons still had at the
Carolingian era a quite numerous Jewish
population.

Here, then, is quite enough to support
the conclusion that Merovingian times
knew, thanks to the continuance of Mediterranean shipping and the intermediary of
Marseilles, what we may safely call a great
commerce. It would certainly be an error
to assume that the dealings of the oriental
merchants of Gaul were restricted solely to
articles of luxury. Probably the sale of
jewelry, enamels and silk stuffs resulted in
handsome profits, but this would not be
enough to explain their number and their
extraordinary diffusion throughout all the
country. The traffic of Marseilles was, above
all else, supported by goods for general
consumption such as wine and oil, spices
and papyrus. These commodities, as has
already been pointed out, were regularly
exported to the north.

The oriental merchants of the Frankish
Empire were virtually engaged in wholesale
trade. Their boats, after being discharged
on the quays of Marseilles, certainly carried
back, on leaving the shores of Provence,
not only passengers but return freight. Our
sources of information, to be sure, do not
tell much about the nature of this freight.
Among the possible conjectures, one of the
most likely is that it probably consisted, at

least in good part, in human chattels — that is to say, in slaves. Traffic in slaves did not cease to be carried on in the Frankish Empire until the end of the ninth century. The wars waged against the barbarians of Saxony, Thuringia and the Slavic regions provided a source of supply which seems to have been abundant enough. Gregory of Tours speaks of Saxon slaves belonging to a merchant of Orleans, and it is a good guess that this Samo, who departed in the first half of the seventh century with a band of companions for the country of Wends, whose king he eventually became, was very probably nothing more than an adventurer trafficking in slaves. And it is of course obvious that the slave trade, to which the Jews still assiduously applied themselves in the ninth century, must have had its origin in an earlier era.

If the bulk of the commerce in Merovingian Gaul was to be found in the hands of oriental merchants, their influence, however, should not be exaggerated. Side by side with them, and according to all indications in constant relations with them, are mentioned indigenous merchants. Gregory of Tours does not fail to supply information concerning them, which would undoubtedly have been more voluminous if his narrative had had more than a merely incidental interest in them. He shows the king consenting to a loan to the merchants of Verdun, whose business prospers so well that they soon find themselves in a position to reimburse him. He mentions the existence in Paris of a *domus negociantum* — that is to say, apparently, of a sort of market or bazaar. He speaks of a merchant profiteering during the great famine of 585 and getting rich. And in all these anecdotes he is dealing, without the least doubt, with professionals and not with merely casual buyers or sellers.

The picture which the commerce of Merovingian Gaul presents is repeated, naturally, in the other maritime Germanic kingdoms of the Mediterranean — among the Ostrogoths of Italy, among the Vandals of Africa, among the Visigoths of Spain.

The Edict of Theodoric contained a quantity of stipulations relative to merchants. Carthage continued to be an important port in close relations with Spain, and her ships, apparently, went up the coast as far as Bordeaux. The laws of the Visigoths mentioned merchants from overseas.

In all of this is clearly manifest the vigorous continuity of the commercial development of the Roman Empire after the Germanic invasions. They did not put an end to the economic unity of antiquity. By means of the Mediterranean and the relations kept up thereby between the West and the East, this unity, on the contrary, was preserved with a remarkable distinctiveness. The great inland sea of Europe no longer belonged, as before, to a single State. But nothing yet gave reason to predict that it would soon cease to have its time-honored importance. Despite the transformations which it had undergone, the new world had not lost the Mediterranean character of the old. On the shores of the sea was still concentrated the better part of its activities. No indication yet gave warning of the end of the commonwealth of civilization, created by the Roman Empire from the Pillars of Hercules to the Aegean Sea. At the beginning of the seventh century, anyone who sought to look into the future would have been unable to discern any reason for not believing in the continuance of the old tradition.

Yet what was then natural and reasonable to predict was not to be realized. The world-order which had survived the Germanic invasions was not able to survive the invasion of Islam.

It is thrown across the path of history with the elemental force of a cosmic cataclysm. Even in the lifetime of Mahomet (571–632) no one could have imagined the consequences or have prepared for them. Yet the movement took no more than fifty years to spread from the China Sea to the Atlantic Ocean. Nothing was able to withstand it. At the first blow, it overthrew the Persian Empire (637–644). It took from the Byzantine Empire, in quick succession,

Syria (634–636), Egypt (640–642), Africa (698). It reached into Spain (711). The resistless advance was not to slow down until the start of the eighth century, when the walls of Constantinople on the one side (713) and the soldiers of Charles Martel on the other (732) broke that great enveloping offensive against the two flanks of Christianity.

But if its force of expansion was exhausted, it had none the less changed the face of the world. Its sudden thrust had destroyed ancient Europe. It had put an end to the Mediterranean commonwealth in which it had gathered its strength.

The familiar and almost "family" sea which once united all the parts of this commonwealth was to become a barrier between them. On all its shores, for cen-turies, social life, in its fundamental characteristics, had been the same; religion, the same; customs and ideas, the same or very nearly so. The invasion of the barbarians from the North had modified nothing essential in that situation.

But now, all of a sudden, the very lands where civilization had been born were torn away; the Cult of the Prophet was substituted for the Christian Faith, Moslem law for Roman law, the Arab tongue for the Greek and the Latin tongue.

The Mediterranean had been a Roman lake; it now became, for the most part, a Moslem lake. From this time on it separated, instead of uniting, the East and the West of Europe. The tie which was still binding the Byzantine Empire to the Germanic kingdoms of the West was broken.

The Ninth Century

The tremendous effect the invasion of Islam had upon Western Europe has not, perhaps, been fully appreciated.

Out of it arose a new and unparalleled situation, unlike anything that had gone before. Through the Phoenicians, the Greeks, and finally the Romans, Western Europe had always received the cultural stamp of the East. It had lived, as it were, by virtue of the Mediterranean; now for the first time it was forced to live by its own resources. The center of gravity, heretofore on the shore of the Mediterranean, was shifted to the north. As a result the Frankish Empire, which had so far been playing only a minor rôle in the history of Europe, was to become the arbiter of Europe's destinies.

There is obviously more than mere coincidence in the simultaneity of the closing of the Mediterranean by Islam and the entry of the Carolingians on the scene. There is the distinct relation of cause and effect between the two. The Frankish Empire was fated to lay the foundations of the Europe of the Middle Ages. But the mission which it fulfilled had as an essential prior condition the overthrow of the traditional world-order. The Carolingians would never have been called upon to play the part they did if historical evolution had not been turned aside from its course and, so to speak, "de-Saxoned" by the Moslem invasion. Without Islam, the Frankish Empire would probably never have existed and Charlemagne, without Mahomet, would be inconceivable.

This is made plain enough by the many contrasts between the Merovingian era, during which the Mediterranean retained its time-honored historical importance, and the Carolingian era, when that influence ceased to make itself felt. These contrasts were in evidence everywhere: in religious sentiment, in political and social institutions, in literature, in language and even in handwriting. From whatever standpoint it is studied, the civilization of the ninth century shows a distinct break with the civilization of antiquity. Nothing would be more fallacious than to see therein a simple continuation of the preceding centuries. The *coup d'état* of Pepin the Short was considerably more than the substitution of one dynasty for another. It marked a new orientation of the course hitherto followed by history. At first glance there seems reason to believe that Charlemagne, in assuming the title of Roman Emperor and of Augustus, wished to restore the ancient tradition. In reality, in setting himself up against the Emperor of Constantinople, he broke that tradition. His Empire was Roman only in so far as the Catholic Church was Roman. For it was from the Church, and the Church alone, that came its inspiration. The forces which he placed at her service were, moreover, forces of the north. His principal collaborators, in religious and cultural matters, were no longer, as they had previously been, Italians, Aquitanians, or Spaniards; they were Anglo-Saxons — a St. Boniface or an Alcuin — or they were Swabians, like Einhard. In the affairs of the State, which was now cut off from the Mediterranean, southerners played scarcely any rôle. The Germanic influence commenced to dominate at the very moment when the Frankish Empire, forced to turn away from the Mediterranean, spread over Northern Europe and pushed its frontiers as far as the Elbe and the mountains of Bohemia.[1]

In the field of economics the contrast, which the Carolingian period shows to Merovingian times, is especially striking. In the days of the Merovingians, Gaul was still a maritime country and trade and traffic flourished because of that fact. The Empire of Charlemagne, on the contrary, was essentially an inland one. No longer was there any communication with the exterior; it was a closed State, a State without foreign markets, living in a condition of almost complete isolation.

[1] The objection may be raised that Charlemagne conquered in Italy the kingdom of the Lombards and in Spain the region included between the Pyrenees and the Ebro. But these thrusts towards the south are by no means to be explained by a desire to dominate the shores of the Mediterranean. The expeditions against the Lombards were provoked by political causes and especially by the alliance with the Papacy. The expedition in Spain had no other aim than the establishing of a solid frontier against the Moslems.

To be sure, the transition from one era to the other was not clear-cut. The trade of Marseilles did not suddenly cease but, from the middle of the seventh century, waned gradually as the Moslems advanced in the Mediterranean. Syria, conquered by them in 633–638, no longer kept it thriving with her ships and her merchandise. Shortly afterwards, Egypt passed in her turn under the yoke of Islam (638–640), and papyrus no longer came to Gaul. A characteristic consequence is that, after 677, the royal chancellery stopped using papyrus. The importation of spices kept up for a while, for the monks of Corbie, in 716, believed it useful to have ratified for the last time their privileges of the *tonlieu* of Fos. A half century later, solitude reigned in the port of Marseilles. Her foster-mother, the sea, was shut off from her and the economic life of the inland regions which had been nourished through her intermediary was definitely extinguished. By the ninth century Provence, once the richest country of Gaul, had become the poorest.

More and more, the Moslems consolidated their domination over the sea. In the course of the ninth century they seized the Balearic Isles, Corsica, Sardinia, Sicily. On the coasts of Africa they founded new ports: Tunis (698–703); later on, Mehdia to the south of this city; then Cairo, in 973. Palermo, where stood a great arsenal, became their principal base in the Tyrrhenian Sea. Their fleets sailed it in complete mastery; commercial flotillas transported the products of the West to Cairo, whence they were redispatched to Bagdad, or pirate fleets devastated the coasts of Provence and Italy and put towns to the torch after they had been pillaged and their inhabitants captured to be sold as slaves. In 889 a band of these plunderers even laid hold of Fraxinetum (the present Garde-Frainet, in the Department of the Var) not far from Nice, the garrison of which, for nearly a century thereafter, subjected the neighboring populace to continual raids and menaced the roads which led across the Alps from France to Italy.

The efforts of Charlemagne and his successors to protect the coasts from Saracen raiders were as impotent as their attempts to oppose the invasions of the Norsemen in the north and west. The hardihood and seamanship of the Danes and Norwegians made it easy for them to plunder the coasts of the Carolingian Empire during the whole of the eleventh century. They conducted their raids not only from the North Sea, the Channel, and the Gulf of Gascony, but at times even from the Mediterranean. Every river which emptied into these seas was, at one time or another, ascended by their skilfully constructed barks, splendid specimens whereof, brought to light by recent excavations, are now preserved at Oslo. Periodically the valleys of the Rhine, the Meuse, the Scheldt, the Seine, the Loire, the Garonne and the Rhône were the scene of systematic and persistent pillaging. The devastation was so complete that, in many cases indeed, the population itself disappeared. And nothing is a better illustration of the essentially inland character of the Frankish Empire than its inability to organize the defense of its coasts, against either Saracens or Norsemen. For that defense, to be effective, should have been a naval defense, and the Empire had no fleets, or hastily improvised ones at best.

Such conditions were incompatible with the existence of a commerce of first-rate importance. The historical literature of the ninth century contains, it is true, certain references to merchants (*mercatores, negociatores*), but no illusion should be cherished as to their importance. Compared to the number of texts which have been preserved from that era, these references are extremely rare. The capitularies, those regulations touching upon every phase of social life, are remarkably meagre in so far as applies to commerce. From this it may be assumed that the latter played a rôle of only secondary, negligible importance. It was only in the north of Gaul that, during the first half of the ninth century, trade showed any signs of activity.

The ports of Quentovic (a place now vanished, near Etaples in the Department of Pas-de-Calais) and Duurstede (on the Rhine, southwest of Utrecht) which under the Merovingian monarchy were already trading with England and Denmark, seem to have been centers of a widely extended shipping. It is a safe conjecture that because of them the river transport of the Friesians along the Rhine, the Scheldt and the Meuse enjoyed an importance that was matched by no other region during the reigns of Charlemagne and his successors. The cloths woven by the peasants of Flanders, and which contemporary texts designate by the name of Friesian cloaks, together with the wines of Rhenish Germany, supplied to that river traffic the substance of an export trade which seems to have been fairly regular up to the day when the Norsemen took possession of the ports in question. It is known, moreover, that the *deniers* coined at Duurstede had a very extensive circulation. They served as prototypes for the oldest coins of Sweden and Poland, evident proof that they early penetrated, no doubt at the hands of the Norsemen, as far as the Baltic Sea. Attention may also be called, as having been the substance of a rather extensive trade, to the salt industry of Noirmoutier, where Irish ships were to be seen. Salzburg salt, on the other hand, was shipped along the Danube and its affluents to the interior of the Empire. The sale of slaves, despite the prohibitions that were laid down by the sovereigns, was carried on along the western frontiers, where the prisoners of war taken from among the pagan Slavs found numerous purchasers.

The Jews seem to have applied themselves particularly to this sort of traffic. They were still numerous, and were found in every part of Francia. Those in the south of Gaul were in close relations with their coreligionists of Moslem Spain, to whom they are accused of having sold Christian children.

It was probably from Spain, or perhaps also from Venice, that these Jews obtained the spices and the valuable textiles in which they dealt. However, the obligation to which they were subjected of having their children baptized must have caused a great number of them to emigrate south of the Pyrenees at an early date, and their commercial importance steadily declined in the course of the ninth century. As for the Syrians, they were no longer of importance at this era.

It is, then, most likely that the commerce of Carolingian times was very much reduced. Except in the neighborhood of Quentovic and Duurstede, it consisted only in the transport of indispensable commodities, such as wine and salt, in the prohibited traffic of a few slaves, and in the barter, through the intermediary of the Jews, of a small number of products from the East.

Of a regular and normal commercial activity, of steady trading carried on by a class of professional merchants, in short, of all that constitutes the very essence of an economy of exchange worthy of the name, no traces are to be found after the closing off of the Mediterranean by the Islamic invasion. The great number of markets, which were to be found in the ninth century, in no way contradicts this assertion. They were, as a matter of fact, only small local marketplaces, instituted for the weekly provisioning of the populace by means of the retail sale of foodstuffs from the country. As a proof of the commercial activity of the Carolingian era, it would be equally beside the point to speak of the existence of the street occupied by merchants at Aix-la-Chapelle near the palace of Charlemagne, or of similar streets near certain great abbeys such as, for example, that of St. Riquier. The merchants with whom we have to do here were not, in fact, professional merchants but servitors charged with the duty of supplying the Court or the monks. They were, so to speak, employees of the seignorial household staff and were in no respect merchants.

There is, moreover, material proof of the economic decline which affected Western Europe from the day when she ceased to belong to the Mediterranean commonwealth. It is furnished by the reform of the monetary system, initiated by Pepin the Short and completed by Charlemagne. That reform abandoned gold coinage and substituted silver in its place. The *solidus* which had heretofore, conforming to the Roman tradition, constituted the basic monetary unit, was now only nominal money. The only real coins from this time on were the silver *deniers*, weighing about two grams, the metallic value of which, compared to that of the dollar, was approximately eight and one-half cents. The metallic value of the Merovingian gold *solidus* being nearly three dollars, the importance of the reform can be readily appreciated. Undoubtedly it is to be explained only by a prodigious falling off of both trading and wealth.

If it is admitted, and it must be admitted, that the reappearance of gold coinage, with the florins of Florence and the ducats of Venice in the thirteenth century, characterized the economic renaissance of Europe, the inverse is also true: the abandoning of gold coinage in the eighth century was the manifestation of a profound decline. It is not enough to say that Pepin and Charlemagne wished to remedy the monetary disorder of the last days of the Merovingian era. It would have been quite possible for them to find a remedy without giving up the gold standard. They gave up the standard, obviously, from necessity — that is to say, as a result of the disappearance of the yellow metal in Gaul. And this disappearance had no other cause than the interruption of the commerce of the Mediterranean. The proof of this is given by the fact that Southern Italy, remaining in contact with Constantinople, retained like the latter a gold standard, for which the Carolingian sovereigns were forced to substitute a silver standard. The very light weight of their *deniers,* moreover, testifies to the economic isolation of their Empire. It is inconceivable that they would have reduced the monetary unit to a thirtieth of its former value if there had been preserved the slightest bond between their States and the Mediterranean regions where the gold *solidus* continued to circulate.

But this is not all. The monetary reform of the ninth century not only was in keeping with the general impoverishment of the era in which it took place, but with the circulation of money which was noteworthy for both lightness and inadequacy. In the absence of centers of attraction sufficiently powerful to draw money from afar, it remained, so to speak, stagnant. Charlemagne and his successors in vain ordered that *deniers* should be coined only in the royal mints. Under the reign of Louis the Pious, it was necessary to give to certain churches authorization to coin money, in view of the difficulties, under which they labored, of obtaining cash. From the second half of the ninth century on, the authorization to establish a market was almost always accompanied by the authorization to establish a mint in the same place. The State could not retain the monopoly of minting coins. It was consistently frittered away. And that is again a manifestation, by no means equivocal, of the economic decline. History shows that the better commerce is sustained, the more the monetary system is centralized and simplified. The dispersion, the variety, and in fact the anarchy which it manifests as we follow the course of the ninth century, ends by giving striking confirmation to the general theory here put forward.

There have been some attempts to attribute to Charlemagne a far-seeing political economy. This is to lend him ideas which, however great we suppose his genius to have been, it is impossible for him to have had. No one can submit with any likelihood of truth that the projects which he commenced in 793, to join the Rednitz to the Altmühl and so establish communication between the Rhine and the Danube, could have had any other purpose than the transport of troops, or that the wars against the Avars were provoked by the desire to open up a commercial route to Constantinople. The stipulations, in other respects inoperative, of the capitularies regarding coinages, weights and measures, the market-tolls and the markets, were inti-

mately bound up with the general system of regulation and control which was typical of Carolingian legislation. The same is true regarding the measures taken against usury and the prohibition enjoining members of the clergy from engaging in business. Their purpose was to combat fraud, disorder and indiscipline and to impose a Christian morality on the people. Only a prejudiced point of view can see in them an attempt to stimulate the economic development of the Empire.

We are so accustomed to consider the reign of Charlemagne as an era of revival that we are unconsciously led to imagine an identical progress in all fields. Unfortunately, what is true of literary culture, of the religious State, of customs, institutions and statecraft is not true of communications and commerce. Every great thing that Charlemagne accomplished was accomplished either by his military strength or by his alliance with the Church. For that matter, neither the Church nor arms could overcome the circumstances in virtue of which the Frankish Empire found itself deprived of foreign markets. It was forced, in fact, to accommodate itself to a situation which was inevitably prescribed. History is obliged to recognize that, however brilliant it seems in other respects, the cycle of Charlemagne, considered from an economic viewpoint, is a cycle of regression.

The financial organization of the Frankish Empire makes this plain. It was, indeed, as rudimentary as could be. The poll tax, which the Merovingians had preserved in imitation of Rome, no longer existed. The resources of the sovereign consisted only in the revenue from his demesnes, in the tributes levied on conquered tribes and in the booty got by war. The market-tolls no longer contributed to the replenishment of the treasury, thus attesting to the commercial decline of the period. They were nothing more than a simple extortion brutally levied in kind on the infrequent merchandise transported by the rivers or along the roads. The sorry proceeds, which should have served to keep up the bridges, the docks and the highways, were swallowed up by the functionaries who collected them. The *missi dominici*, created to supervise their administration, were impotent in abolishing the abuses which they proved to exist because the State, unable to pay its agents, was likewise unable to impose its authority on them. It was obliged to call on the aristocracy which, thanks to their social status, alone could give free services. But in so doing it was constrained, for lack of money, to choose the instruments of power from among the midst of a group of men whose most evident interest was to diminish that power. The recruiting of the functionaries from among the aristocracy was the fundamental vice of the Frankish Empire and the essential cause of its dissolution, which became so rapid after the death of Charlemagne. Surely, nothing is more fragile than that State the sovereign of which, all-powerful in theory, is dependent in fact upon the fidelity of his independent agents.

The feudal system was in embryo in this contradictory situation. The Carolingian Empire would have been able to keep going only if it had possessed, like the Byzantine Empire or the Empire of the Caliphs, a tax system, a financial control, a fiscal centralization and a treasury providing for the salary of functionaries, for public works, and for the maintenance of the army and the navy. The financial impotence which caused its downfall was a clear demonstration of the impossibility it encountered of maintaining a political structure on an economic base which was no longer able to support the load.

That economic base of the State, as of society, was from this time on the landed proprietor. Just as the Carolingian Empire was an inland State without foreign markets, so also was it an essentially agricultural State. The traces of commerce which were still to be found there were negligible. There was no other property than landed property, and no other work than rural work. As has already been stated above, this predominance of agriculture was no new fact. It existed in a very distinct form in the Roman era and it continued with increasing strength in the Merovingian era. As early as the close of antiquity, all the west of Europe was covered with great demesnes belonging to an aristocracy the members of which bore the title of senators. More and more, property was disappearing in a transformation into hereditary tenures, while the old free farmers were themselves undergoing a transformation into "cultivators" bound to the soil, from father to son. The Germanic invasions did not noticeably alter this state of things. We have definitely given up the idea of picturing the Germanic tribes in the light of a democracy of peasants, all on an equal footing. Social distinctions were very great among them even when they first invaded the Empire. They comprised a minority of the wealthy and a majority of the poor. The number of slaves and half-free was considerable.

The arrival of the invaders in the Roman provinces brought with it, then, no overthrow of the existing order. The newcomers preserved, in adapting themselves thereto, the status quo. Many of the invaders received from the king or acquired by force or by marriage, or otherwise, great demesnes which made them the equals of the "senators." The landed aristocracy, far from disappearing, was on the contrary invigorated by new elements.

The disappearance of the small free proprietors continued. It seems, in fact, that as early as the start of the Carolingian period only a very small number of them still existed in Gaul. Charlemagne in vain took measures to safeguard those who were left. The need of protection inevitably made them turn to the more powerful individuals to whose patronage they subordinated their persons and their possessions.

Large estates, then, kept on being more and more generally in evidence after the period of the invasions. The favor which the kings showed the Church was an additional factor in this development, and the religious fervor of the aristocracy had the same effect. Monasteries, whose number multiplied with such remarkable rapidity after the seventh century, were receiving bountiful gifts of land. Everywhere ecclesiastical demesnes and lay demesnes were mixed up together, uniting not only cultivated ground, but woods, heaths and wastelands.

The organization of these demesnes remained in conformity, in Frankish Gaul, with what it had been in Roman Gaul. It is clear that this could not have been otherwise. The Germanic tribes had no motive for, and were, furthermore, incapable of, substituting a different organization. It consisted, in its essentials, of classifying all the land in two groups, subject to two distinct forms of government. The first, the less extensive, was directly exploited by the proprietor; the second was divided, under deeds of tenure, among the peasants. Each of the *villae* of which a demesne was composed comprised both seignorial land and censal land, divided in units of cultivation held by hereditary right by manants or villeins in return for the prestation of rents, in money or in kind, and statute-labor.

As long as urban life and commerce flourished, the great demesnes had a market for the disposal of their produce. There is no room for doubt that during all the Merovingian era it was through them that the city groups were provisioned and that the merchants were supplied. But it could not help be otherwise when trade disappeared and therewith the merchant class and the municipal population. The great estates suffered the same fate as the Frankish Empire. Like it, they lost their markets. The possibility of selling abroad existed no longer because of the lack of buyers, and it became useless to continue to produce more than the indispensable minimum for the subsistence of the men, proprietors or tenants, living on the estate.

For an economy of exchange was substituted an economy of consumption. Each demesne, in place of continuing to deal with the outside, constituted from this time on a little world of its own. It lived by itself and for itself, in the traditional immo-

bility of a patriarchal form of government. The ninth century is the golden age of what we have called the closed domestic economy and which we might call, with more exactitude, the economy of no markets.

This economy, in which production had no other aim than the sustenance of the demesnial group and which in consequence was absolutely foreign to the idea of profit, can not be considered as a natural and spontaneous phenomenon. It was, on the contrary, merely the result of an evolution which forced it to take this characteristic form. The great proprietors did not give up selling the products of their lands of their own free will; they stopped because they could not do otherwise. Certainly if commerce had continued to supply them regularly with the means of disposing of these products abroad, they would not have neglected to profit thereby. They did not sell because they could not sell, and they could not sell because markets were wanting. The closed demesnial organization, which made its appearance at the beginning of the ninth century, was a phenomenon due to compulsion. That is merely to say that it was an abnormal phenomenon.

This can be most effectively shown by comparing the picture, which Carolingian Europe presents, with that of Southern Russia at the same era.

We know that bands of sea-faring Norsemen, that is to say of Scandinavians originally from Sweden, established their domination over the Slavs of the watershed of the Dnieper during the course of the ninth century. These conquerors, whom the conquered designated by the name of Russians, naturally had to congregate in groups in order to insure their safety in the midst of the populations they had subjected.

For this purpose they built fortified enclosures, called *gorods* in the Slavic tongue, where they settled with their princes and the images of their gods. The most ancient Russian cities owe their origin to these entrenched camps. There were such camps at Smolensk, Suzdal and Novgorod; the most important and the most civilized was at Kiev, the prince of which ranked above all the other princes. The subsistence of the invaders was assured by tributes levied on the native population.

It was therefore possible for the Russians to live off the land, without seeking abroad to supplement the resources which the country gave them in abundance. They would have done so, without doubt, and been content to use the prestations of their subjects if they had found it impossible, like their contemporaries in Western Europe, to communicate with the exterior. But the position which they occupied must have early led them to practise an economy of exchange.

Southern Russia was placed, as a matter of fact, between two regions of a superior civilization. To the east, beyond the Caspian Sea, extended the Caliphate of Bagdad; to the south, the Black Sea bathed the coasts of the Byzantine Empire and pointed the way towards Constantinople. The barbarians felt at once the effect of these two strong centers of attraction. To be sure, they were in the highest degree energetic, enterprising and adventurous, but their native qualities only served to turn circumstances to the best account. Arab merchants, Jews, and Byzantines were already frequenting the Slavic regions when they took possession, and showed them the route to follow. They themselves did not hesitate to plunge along it under the spur of the love of gain, quite as natural to primitive man as to civilized.

The country they occupied placed at their disposal products particularly well suited for trade with rich empires accustomed to the refinements of life. Its immense forests furnished them with a quantity of honey, precious in those days when sugar was still unknown, and furs, sumptuousness in which was a requisite, even in southern climes, of luxurious dress and equipment.

Slaves were easier still to procure and, thanks to the Moslem harems and the great houses or Byzantine workshops, had a sale as sure as it was remunerative. Thus as early as the ninth century, while the Empire of Charlemagne was kept in isolation after the closing of the Mediterranean, Southern Russia on the contrary was induced to sell her products in the two great markets which exercised their attraction on her. The paganism of the Scandinavians of the Dnieper left them free of the religious scruples which prevented the Christians of the west from having dealings with the Moslems. Belonging neither to the faith of Christ nor to that of Mahomet, they only asked to get rich, in dealing impartially with the followers of either.

The importance of the trade which they kept up as much with the Moslem Empire as with the Greek, is made clear by the extraordinary number of Arab and Byzantine coins discovered in Russia and which mark, like a golden compass needle, the direction of the commercial routes.

In the region of Kiev they followed to the south the course of the Dnieper, to the east the Volga, and to the north the direction marked by the Western Dvina or the lakes which abut the Gulf of Bothnia. Information from Jewish or Arab travellers and from Byzantine writers fortunately supplements the data from archaeological records. It will suffice here to give a brief résumé of what Constantine Porphyrogenetus[2] reports in the ninth century. He shows the Russians assembling their boats at Kiev each year after the ice melts. Their flotilla slowly descends the Dnieper, whose numerous cataracts present obstacles that have to be avoided by dragging the barks along the banks. The sea once reached, they sail before the wind along the coasts towards Constantinople, the supreme goal of their long and perilous voyage. There the Russian merchants had a special quarter and made commercial treaties, the oldest of which dates back to the ninth century, regulating their relations with the population. Many of them, seduced by its attractions, settled down there and took service in the Imperial

[2] Byzantine Emperor (912–959) and scholar who wrote or inspired several works which provide much of our knowledge of his time. [Editor's note]

Guard, as had done, before that time, the Germans in the legions of Rome.

The City of the Emperors (*Czarograd*) had for the Russians a fascination the influence of which has lasted across the centuries. It was from her that they received Christianity (957–1015); it was from her that they borrowed their art, their writing, the use of money and a good part of their administrative organization. Nothing more is needed to demonstrate the rôle played by Byzantine commerce in their social life. It occupied so essential a place therein that without it their civilization would remain inexplicable. To be sure, the forms in which it is found are very primitive, but the important thing is not the forms of this traffic; it is the effect it had.

Among the Russians of the late Middle Ages it actually determined the constitution of society. By striking contrast with what has been shown to be the case with their contemporaries of Carolingian Europe, not only the importance but the very idea of real estate was unknown to them. Their notion of wealth comprised only personal property, of which slaves were the most valuable. They were not interested in land except in so far as, by their control of it, they were able to appropriate its products. And if this conception was that of a class of warrior-conquerors, there is but little doubt that it was held for so long because these warriors were, at the same time, merchants. We might, incidentally, add that the concentration of the Russians in the *gorods,* motivated in the beginning by military necessity, is itself found to fit in admirably with commercial needs. An organization created by barbarians for the purpose of keeping conquered populations under the yoke was well adapted to the sort of life which theirs became after they gave heed to the economic attraction of Byzantium and Bagdad. Their example shows that a society does not necessarily have to pass through an agrarian stage before giving itself over to commerce. Here commerce appears as an original phenomenon. And if this is so, it is because the Russians instead

of finding themselves isolated from the outside world like Western Europe were on the contrary pushed or, to use a better word, *drawn* into contact with it from the beginning. Out of this derive the violent contrasts which are disclosed in comparing their social state with that of the Carolingian Empire: in place of a demesnial aristocracy, a commercial aristocracy; in place of serfs bound to the soil, slaves considered as instruments of work; in place of a population living in the country, a population gathered together in towns; in place, finally, of a simple economy of consumption, an economy of exchange and a regular and permanent commercial activity.

That these outstanding contrasts were the result of circumstances which gave Russia markets while depriving the Carolingian Empire of them, history clearly demonstrates. The activity of Russian trade was maintained, indeed, only as long as the routes to Constantinople and Bagdad remained open before it. It was not fated to withstand the crisis which the Petchenegs brought about in the eleventh century. The invasion of these barbarians along the shores of the Caspian and the Black Seas brought in their train consequences identical to those which the invasion of Islam in the Mediterranean had had for Western Europe in the eighth century.

Just as the latter cut the communications between Gaul and the East, the former cut the communications between Russia and her foreign markets. And in both quarters, the results of this interruption coincide with a singular exactitude. In Russia as in Gaul, when means of communication disappeared and towns were depopulated and the populace forced to find near at hand the means of their subsistence, a period of agricultural economy was substituted for a period of commercial economy. Despite the differences in details, it was the same picture in both cases. The regions of the south, ruined and troubled by the barbarians, gave way in importance to the regions of the north. Kiev fell into a decline as Marseilles had fallen, and the center of the Russian State was removed to Moscow just as the center of the Frankish State, with the Carolingian dynasty, had been removed to the watershed of the Rhine. And to end by making the parallel still more conclusive, there arose, in Russia as in Gaul, a landed aristocracy, and a demesnial system was organized in which the impossibility of exporting or of selling forced production to be limited to the needs of the proprietor and his peasants.

So, in both cases, the same causes produced the same effects. But they did not produce them at the same date. Russia was living by trade at an era when the Carolingian Empire knew only the demesnial régime, and she in turn inaugurated this form of government at the very moment when Western Europe, having found new markets, broke away from it. We shall examine further how this break was accomplished. It will suffice for the moment to have proved, by the example of Russia, the theory that the economy of the Carolingian era was not the result of an internal evolution but must be attributed to the closing of the Mediterranean by Islam.

From *MOHAMMED AND CHARLEMAGNE*

HENRI PIRENNE

Western Europe before Islam

FROM whatever standpoint we regard it, then, the period inaugurated by the establishment of the Barbarians within the Empire introduced no absolute historical innovation.[1] What the Germans destroyed was not the Empire, but the Imperial government *in partibus occidentis*. They themselves acknowledged as much by installing themselves as *foederati*. Far from seeking to replace the Empire by anything new, they established themselves within it, and although their settlement was accompanied by a process of serious degradation, they did not introduce a new scheme of government; the ancient *palazzo*, so to speak, was divided up into apartments, but it still survived as a building. In short, the essential character of "Romania" still remained Mediterranean. The frontier territories, which remained Germanic, and England, played no part in it as yet; it is a mistake to regard them at this period as a point of departure. Considering matters as they actually were, we see that the great novelty of the epoch was a political fact: in the Occident a plurality of States had replaced the unity of the Roman State. And this, of course, was a very considerable novelty. The aspect of Europe was changing, but the fundamental character of its life remained the same. These States, which have been described as national States, were not really national at all, but were merely fragments of the great unity which they had replaced. There was no profound transformation except in Britain.

There the Emperor and the civilization of the Empire had disappeared. Nothing remained of the old tradition. A new world had made its appearance. The old law and language and institutions were replaced by those of the Germans. A civilization of a new type was manifesting itself, which we may call the Nordic or Germanic civilization. It was completely opposed to the Mediterranean civilization syncretized in the Late Empire, that last form of antiquity. Here was no trace of the Roman State with its legislative ideal, its civil population, and its Christian religion, but a society which had preserved the blood tie between its members; the family community, with all the consequences which it entailed in law and morality and economy; a paganism like that of the heroic poems; such were the things that constituted the originality of these Barbarians, who had thrust back the ancient world in order to take its place. In Britain a new age was beginning, which did not gravitate towards the South. The man of the North had conquered and taken for his own this extreme corner of that "Romania" of which he had no memories, whose majesty he repudiated, and to which

[1] These things were retained: the language, the currency, writing (papyrus), weights and measures, the kinds of foodstuffs in common use, the social classes, the religion — the role of Arianism has been exaggerated — art, the law, the administration, the taxes, the economic organization. [Pirenne's note]

From Henri Pirenne, *Mohammed and Charlemagne* (London, 1939), pp. 140–144, 147–150, 265–285. By permission of George Allen & Unwin Ltd.

he owed nothing. In every sense of the word he replaced it, and in replacing it he destroyed it.

The Anglo-Saxon invaders came into the Empire fresh from their Germanic environment, and had never been subjected to the influences of Rome. Further, the province of Britain, in which they had established themselves, was the least Romanized of all the provinces. In Britain, therefore, they remained themselves: the Germanic, Nordic, Barbarian soul of peoples whose culture might almost be called Homeric has been the essential factor in the history of this country.

But the spectacle presented by this Anglo-Saxon Britain was unique. We should seek in vain for anything like it on the Continent. There "Romania" still existed, except on the frontier, or along the Rhine, in the decumate lands, and along the Danube — that is to say, in the provinces of Germania, Raetia, Noricum and Pannonia, all close to that Germania whose inhabitants had overflowed into the Empire and driven it before them. But these border regions played no part of their own, since they were attached to States which had been established, like that of the Franks or the Ostrogoths, in the heart of "Romania." And there it is plain that the old state of affairs still existed. The invaders, too few in number, and also too long in contact with the Empire were inevitably absorbed, and they asked nothing better. What may well surprise us is that there was so little Germanism in the new States, all of which were ruled by Germanic dynasties. Language, religion, institutions and art were entirely, or almost entirely, devoid of Germanism. We find some Germanic influences in the law of those countries situated to the north of the Seine and the Alps, but until the Lombards arrived in Italy these did not amount to very much. If some have held a contrary belief, it is because they have followed the Germanic school and have wrongly applied to Gaul, Italy, and Spain what they find in the *Leges Barbarorum* of the Salians, the Ripuarians and the

Bavarians. They have also extended to the period which preceded the Carolingians what is true only of the latter. Moreover, they have exaggerated the role of Merovingian Gaul by allowing themselves to be governed by the thought of what it later became, but as yet was not.

What was Clovis as compared with Theodoric? And let it be noted that after Clovis the Frankish kings, despite all their efforts, could neither establish themselves in Italy, nor even recapture the Narbonnaise from the Visigoths. It is evident that they were tending towards the Mediterranean. The object of their conquest beyond the Rhine was to defend their kingdom against the Barbarians, and was far from having the effect of Germanizing it. But to admit that under the conditions of their establishment in the Empire, and with the small forces which they brought with them, the Visigoths, Burgundi, Ostrogoths, Vandals and Franks could have intended to Germanize the Empire is simply to admit the impossible.

Moreover, we must not forget the part played by the Church, within which Rome had taken refuge, and which, in imposing itself upon the Barbarians, was at the same time imposing Rome upon them. In the Occident, in the Roman world which had become so disordered as a State, the Germanic kings were, so to speak, points of political crystallization. But the old, or shall we say, the classic social equilibrium still existed in the world about them, though it had suffered inevitable losses.

In other words, the Mediterranean unity which was the essential feature of this ancient world was maintained in all its various manifestations. The increasing Hellenization of the Orient did not prevent it from continuing to influence the Occident by its commerce, its art, and the vicissitudes of its religious life. To a certain extent, as we have seen, the Occident was becoming Byzantinized.

And this explains Justinian's impulse of reconquest, which almost restored the Mediterranean to the status of a Roman lake.

And regarding it from our point of view, it is, of course, plainly apparent that this Empire could not last. But this was not the view of its contemporaries. The Lombard invasion was certainly less important than has been supposed. The striking thing about it is its tardiness.

Justinian's Mediterranean policy — and it really was a Mediterranean policy, since he sacrificed to this policy his conflicts with the Persians and the Slavs — was in tune with the Mediterranean spirit of European civilization as a whole from the 5th to the 7th century. It is on the shores of this *mare nostrum* that we find all the specific manifestations of the life of the epoch. Commerce gravitated toward the sea, as under the Empire; there the last representatives of the ancient literature — Boëtius, Cassiodorus — wrote their works; there, with Caesarius of Arles, and Gregory the Great, the new literature of the Church was born and began to develop; there writers like Isidore of Seville made the inventory of civilization from which the Middle Ages obtained their knowledge of antiquity; there, at Lérins, or at Monte Cassino, monasticism, coming from the Orient, was acclimatized to its Occidental environment; from the shores of the Mediterranean came the missionaries who converted England, and it was there that arose the characteristic monuments of that Hellenistico-Oriental art which seemed destined to become the art of the Occident, as it had remained that of the Orient.

There was as yet nothing, in the 7th century, that seemed to announce the end of the community of civilization established by the Roman Empire from the Pillars of Hercules to the Aegean Sea and from the shores of Egypt and Africa to those of Italy, Gaul, and Spain. The new world had not lost the Mediterranean character of the ancient world. All its activities were concentrated and nourished on the shores of the Mediterranean.

There was nothing to indicate that the millenary evolution of society was to be suddenly interrupted. No one was anticipating a catastrophe. Although the immediate successors of Justinian were unable to continue his work, they did not repudiate it. They refused to make any concession to the Lombards; they feverishly fortified Africa; they established their themes there as in Italy; their policies took account of the Franks and the Visigoths alike; their fleet controlled the sea; and the Pope of Rome regarded them as his Sovereigns.

The greatest intellect of the Occident, Gregory the Great, Pope from 590 to 604, saluted the Emperor Phocas, in 603, as reigning only over free men, while the kings of the Occident reigned only over slaves. . . .

The expansion of Islam in the Mediterranean basin

THE ISLAMIC INVASION

Nothing could be more suggestive, nothing could better enable us to comprehend the expansion of Islam in the 7th century, than to compare its effect upon the Roman Empire with that of the Germanic invasions. These latter invasions were the climax of a situation which was as old as the Empire, and indeed even older, and which had weighed upon it more or less heavily throughout its history. When the Empire, its frontiers penetrated, abandoned the struggle, the invaders promptly allowed themselves to become absorbed in it, and as far as possible they maintained its civilization, and entered into the community upon which this civilization was based.

On the other hand, before the Mohammedan epoch the Empire had had practically no dealings with the Arabian peninsula. It contented itself with building a wall to protect Syria against the nomadic bands of the desert, much as it had built a wall in the north of Britain in order to check the invasions of the Picts; but this Syrian *limes*, some remains of which may still be seen on crossing the desert, was in no way comparable to that of the Rhine or the Danube.

The Empire had never regarded this as one of its vulnerable points, nor had it ever massed there any large proportion of its military forces. It was a frontier of inspection, which was crossed by the caravans that brought perfumes and spices. The Persian Empire, another of Arabia's neighbours, had taken the same precaution. After all, there was nothing to fear from the nomadic Bedouins of the Peninsula, whose civilization was still in the tribal stage, whose religious beliefs were hardly better than fetichism, and who spent their time in making war upon one another, or pillaging the caravans that travelled from south to north, from Yemen to Palestine, Syria and the Peninsula of Sinai, passing through Mecca and Yathreb (the future Medina).

Preoccupied by their secular conflict, neither the Roman nor the Persian Empire seems to have had any suspicion of the propaganda by which Mohammed, amidst the confused conflicts of the tribes, was on the point of giving his own people a religion which it would presently cast upon the world, while imposing its own dominion. The Empire was already in deadly danger when John of Damascus was still regarding Islam as a sort of schism, of much the same character as previous heresies.

When Mohammed died, in 632, there was as yet no sign of the peril which was to manifest itself in so overwhelming a fashion a couple of years later. No measures had been taken to defend the frontier. It is evident that whereas the Germanic menace had always attracted the attention of the Emperors, the Arab onslaught took them by surprise. In a certain sense, the expansion of Islam was due to chance, if we can give this name to the unpredictable consequence of a combination of causes. The success of the attack is explained by the exhaustion of the two Empires which marched with Arabia, the Roman and the Persian, at the end of the long struggle between them, which had at last culmi-

nated in the victory of Heraclius over Chosröes (d. 627).

Byzantium had just reconquered its prestige, and its future seemed assured by the fall of the secular enemy and the restoration to the Empire of Syria, Palestine and Egypt. The Holy Cross, which had long ago been carried off, was now triumphantly restored to Constantinople by the conqueror. The sovereign of India sent his felicitations, and the king of the Franks, Dagobert, concluded a perpetual peace with him. After this it was natural to expect that Heraclius would continue the Occidental policy of Justinian. It was true that the Lombards had occupied a portion of Italy, and the Visigoths, in 624, recaptured from Byzantium its last outposts in Spain; but what was that compared with the tremendous recovery which had just been accomplished in the Orient?

However, the effort, which was doubtless excessive, had exhausted the Empire. The provinces which Persia had just surrendered were suddenly wrested from the Empire by Islam. Heraclius (610–641) was doomed to be a helpless spectator of the first onslaught of this new force which was about to disconcert and bewilder the Western world.

The Arab conquest, which brought confusion upon both Europe and Asia, was without precedent. The swiftness of its victory is comparable only with that by which the Mongol Empires of Attila, Jenghiz Khan and Tamerlane were established. But these Empires were as ephemeral as the conquest of Islam was lasting. This religion still has its faithful today in almost every country where it was imposed by the first Caliphs. The lightning-like rapidity of its diffusion was a veritable miracle as compared with the slow progress of Christianity.

By the side of this irruption, what were the conquests, so long delayed, of the Germans, who, after centuries of effort, had succeeded only in nibbling at the edge of "Romania"?

The Arabs, on the other hand, took possession of whole sections of the crumbling Empire. In 634 they seized the Byzantine fortress of Bothra (Bosra) in Transjordania; in 635 Damascus fell before them; in 636 the battle of Yarmok gave them the whole of Syria; in 637 or 638 Jerusalem opened its gates to them, while at the same time their Asiatic conquests included Mesopotamia and Persia. Then it was the turn of Egypt to be attacked; and shortly after the death of Heraclius (641) Alexandria was taken, and before long the whole country was occupied. Next the invasion, still continuing, submerged the Byzantine possessions in North Africa.

All this may doubtless be explained by the fact that the invasion was unexpected, by the disorder of the Byzantine armies, disorganized and surprised by a new method of fighting, by the religious and national discontent of the Monophysites and Nestorians of Syria, to whom the Empire had refused to make any concessions, and of the Coptic Church of Egypt, and by the weakness of the Persians. But all these reasons are insufficient to explain so complete a triumph. The intensity of the results were out of all proportion to the numerical strength of the conquerors. . . .[2]

[2] For further analysis of the Arab conquest the student is referred to the selections from *Medieval Cities* which summarize the more comprehensive treatment in *Mohammed and Charlemagne.* [Editor's note]

MEROVINGIANS AND CAROLINGIANS

POLITICAL ORGANIZATION

Many historians regard what they call the Frankish epoch as constituting an unbroken whole, so that they describe the Carolingian period as the continuation and development of the Merovingian. But in this they are obviously mistaken, and for several reasons.

1st. The Merovingian period belongs to a *milieu* entirely different from that of the Carolingian period. In the 6th and 7th centuries there was still a Mediterranean with which the Merovingians were constantly in touch, and the Imperial tradition still survived in many domains of life.

2nd. The Germanic influence, confined to the vicinity of the Northern frontier, was very feeble, and made itself felt only in certain branches of the law and of procedure.

3rd. Between the more glorious Merovingian period, which lasted until nearly the middle of the 7th century, and the Carolingian period, there was a full century of turbid decadence, in the course of which many of the features of the ancient civilizations disappeared, while others were further elaborated; and it was in this decadence that the Carolingian period had its origin. The ancestors of the Carolingians were not Merovingian kings, but the mayors of the palace. Charlemagne was not in any sense the successor of Dagobert,[3] but of Charles Martel and Pippin.

4th. We must not be confused by the identity of the name *regnum Francorum.* The new kingdom stretched as far as the Elbe and included part of Italy. It contained almost as many Germanic as Romanic populations.

5th. Lastly, its relations with the Church were completely modified. The Merovingian State, like the Roman Empire, was secular. The Merovingian king was *rex Francorum.* The Carolingian king was *Dei gratia rex Francorum,*[4] and this little addition indicates a profound transformation. So great was this transformation that later generations did not realize the significance

[3] Dagobert, Frankish king, ca. 629–639, was the last of the Merovingians to rule as well as reign. [Editor's note]

[4] This had not yet become the regulation formula under Pippin, but it was always employed from the beginning of Charlemagne's reign. Giry, *Manuel de Diplomatique,* p. 318. [Pirenne's note]

of the Merovingian usage. Later copyists and forgers embellished what seemed to them the inadmissible title of the Merovingian kings with a *Dei gratia*.

Thus, the two monarchies — the second of which, as I have endeavoured to show in these pages, was due in some sort to the submersion of the European world by Islam — were far from being continuous, but were mutually opposed.

In the great crisis which led to the collapse of the State founded by Clovis, the Roman foundations crumbled away to nothing.

The first to go was the very conception of the royal power. This, of course, in the form which it assumed under the Merovingians, was not a mere transposition of the Imperial absolutism. I am quite willing to admit that the royal power was, to a great extent, merely a *de facto* despotism. Nevertheless, for the king, as for his subjects, the whole power of the State was concentrated in the monarch.

All that belonged to him was sacred; he could put himself above the law, and no one could gainsay him; he could blind his enemies and confiscate their estates under the pretext that they were guilty of *lèse-majesté*. There was nothing, there was no one that he need consider. The power most resembling his own was that of the Byzantine Emperor, if we take into account the enormous differences due to the unequal levels of the two civilizations.

All the Merovingian administrations preserved, for good or ill, the bureaucratic character of the Roman administration. The Merovingian chancellery, with its lay referendars, was modelled upon that of Rome; the king picked his agents where he chose, even from among his slaves; his bodyguard of *antrustions* was reminiscent of the Pretorian guard. And to tell the truth, the populations over whom he reigned had no conception of any other form of government. It was the government of all the kings of the period, Ostrogothic, Visigothic, Vandal. It should be noted that even when the kings assassinated one another the peoples did not revolt. Ambitious men committed murder, but there were no popular risings.

The cause of the Merovingian decadence was the increasing weakness of the royal power. And this weakness, by which the Carolingians profited, was due to the disorder of the financial administration, and this again was completely Roman. For, as we have seen, the king's treasury was nourished mainly by the impost. And with the disappearance of the gold currency, during the great crisis of the 8th century, this impost also disappeared. The very notion of the public impost was forgotten when the *curiales* of the cities disappeared.

The *monetarii* who forwarded this impost to the treasury in the form of gold *solidi* no longer existed. I think the last mention of them refers to the reign of Pippin. Thus the mayors of the palace no longer received the impost. The monarchy which they established by their *coup d'état* was a monarchy in which the Roman conception of the public impost was abolished.

The kings of the new dynasty, like the kings of the Middle Ages long after them, had no regular resources apart from the revenues of their domains. There were still prestations, of course, which dated from the Roman epoch, and in particular the *tonlieu*. But all these were diminishing. The *droit de gîte* was exercised by the functionaries rather than by the king.[5] As for the *tonlieu*, which brought in less and less as the circulation of goods diminished, the kings made donations of it to the abbeys and the *grandi*.

Some writers have attempted to prove the existence of an impost under the Carolingians. As a matter of fact, there was a custom of annual "gifts" in the Germanic portion of the Empire. And, further, the kings decreed collections and levies of silver at the time of the Norman invasions. But these were expedients which were not continued. In reality, it must be repeated, the basis of the king's financial power was his

5 The *tonlieu* was a market toll; the *droit de gîte* was the feudal right of lodging. [Editor's note]

domain, his fisc, if you will. To this, at least, in the case of Charlemagne, we must add the booty taken in time of war. The ordinary basis of the royal power was purely rural. This was why the mayors of the palace confiscated so many ecclesiastical estates. The king was, and had to remain, if he was to maintain his power, the greatest landowner in the kingdom. No more surveys of lands, no more registers of taxes, no more financial functionaries; hence no more archives, no more offices, no more accounts. The kings no longer had any finances; this, it will be realized, was something new. The Merovingian king bought or paid men with gold; the Carolingian king had to give them fragments of his domain. This was a serious cause of weakness, which was offset by booty as long as the country was at war under Charlemagne, but soon after his reign the consequences made themselves felt. And here, let it be repeated, there was a definite break with the financial tradition of the Romans.

To this first essential difference between the Merovingians and the Carolingians another must be added. The new king, as we have seen, was king by the grace of God. The rite of consecration, introduced under Pippin, made him in some sort a sacerdotal personage. The Merovingian was in every sense a secular king. The Carolingian was crowned only by the intervention of the Church, and the king, by virtue of his consecration, entered into the Church. He had now a religious ideal, and there were limits to his power — the limits imposed by Christian morality. We see that the kings no longer indulged in the arbitrary assassinations and the excesses of personal power which were everyday things in the Merovingian epoch. For proof we have only to read the *De rectoribus Christianis* of Sedulius of Liège, or the *De via regia* of Smaragdus, written, according to Ebert, between 806 and 813.

Through the rite of consecration the Church obtained a hold over the king. Henceforth the secular character of the State was kept in the background. Here

two texts of Hincmar[6] may be cited. "It is to the unction, an episcopal and a spiritual act," he wrote to Charles the Bald in 868; "it is to this benediction, far more than to your earthly power, that you owe the royal dignity." We read further, in the Acts of the Council of Sainte-Macre: "The dignity of the pontiffs is above that of the kings: for the kings are consecrated by the pontiffs, while the pontiffs cannot be consecrated by the kings." After consecration the king owed certain duties to the Church. According to Smaragdus, he had to endeavour with all his might to remedy any defects that had crept into it. But he had also to protect it and to see that the tithe was paid to it.

It will be understood that under these conditions the monarchy acted in association with the Church. We have only to read the Capitularies to realize that these were as much concerned with ecclesiastical discipline and morality as with secular administration.

In the eyes of the Carolingian kings to administer their subjects meant to imbue them with ecclesiastical morality. We have already seen that their economic conceptions were dominated by the Church. The bishops were their councillors and officials. The kings entrusted them with the functions of *missi* and filled their chancellery with clerics. Here is a striking contrast with the Merovingians, who rewarded their lay referendaries by making them bishops. From the time of Hitherius, the first ecclesiastic to enter the chancellery under Charlemagne, no more laymen were employed there for centuries. Bresslau is mistaken in his belief that the invasion of the palace offices by the Church is explained by the fact that the first Carolingians wished to replace the Roman personnel of the Merovingians by an Austrasian personnel, and that they had to engage Austrasian clerics as being the only Austrasians who could

---

[6] Hincmar was a celebrated Archbishop of Rheims, 845–882; Charles the Bald was the West Frankish King, 840–877. [Editor's note]

read and write. No: they wanted to make sure of the collaboration of the Church.

However, it is true that they had to seek men of education among the clerics. During the crisis the education of laymen was discontinued. The mayors themselves were unable to write. The platonic efforts of Charlemagne to spread education among the people came to nothing, and the palace academy had only a few pupils. A period was commencing in which "cleric" and "scholar" were synonymous; hence the importance of the Church, which, in a kingdom where hardly anyone had retained any knowledge of Latin, was able for centuries to impose its language on the administration. We have to make an effort to understand the true significance of this fact; it was tremendous. Here we perceive the appearance of a new medieval characteristic: here was a religious caste which imposed its influence upon the State.

And in addition to this religious caste, the king had to reckon with the military class, which comprised the whole of the lay aristocracy, and all such freemen as had remained independent. Of course, we have glimpses of the rise of this military class under the Merovingian kings. But the aristocracy of the Merovingian epoch was strangely unlike that of the Carolingian era. The great Roman landowners, the *senatores,* whether they resided in the cities or in the country, do not give one the impression that they were primarily soldiers. They were educated. Above all things, they sought employment in the palace or the Church. It is probable that the king recruited his army leaders and the soldiers of his bodyguard more particularly among his Germanic *antrustions.* It is certain that the landowning aristocracy lost no time in attempting to dominate him. But it never succeeded in doing so.

We do not find that the king governed by means of this aristocracy, nor that he allowed it any share in the government as long as he remained powerful. And even though he conferred immunity upon it, he did not surrender either to the aristocracy

or to the churches any of the rights of the crown. As a matter of fact, he had at his disposal two terrible weapons against it: prosecution for *lèse-majesté* and confiscation.

But in order to hold his own against this aristocracy it is obvious that the king had to remain extremely powerful: in other words, extremely wealthy. For the aristocracy — like the Church, for that matter — was constantly increasing its authority over the people. This social development, which began in the days of the late Empire, was continuing. The *grandi* had their private soldiers, numerous *vassi* who had recommended themselves to them (had applied to them for protection), and who constituted a formidable following.

In the Merovingian period the seigneurial authority of the landowners was manifested only within the limits of their private rights. But in the period of anarchy and decadence, when war broke out between the mayors of the palace, who were backed by factions of aristocrats, the institution of vassalage underwent a transformation. It assumed an increasing importance, and its military character became plainly apparent when the Carolingian triumphed over his rivals. From the time of Charles Martel the power exercised by the king was essentially based on his military vassals in the North.

He gave them benefices — that is to say, estates — in exchange for military service, and these estates he confiscated from the churches. "Now," says Guilhiermoz,[7] owing to their importance, these concessions to vassals were henceforth found to tempt, not only persons of mean or moderate condition, but the *great.*"

And this was entirely in the interest of the grantor, who henceforth gave large benefices "on the condition that the concessionaire served him, not only with his own person, but with a number of vassals in proportion to the importance of the benefice conceded." It was undoubtedly by such

---

[7] Guilhiermoz, *Essai sur les origines de la noblesse,* p. 125.

means that Charles Martel was able to recruit the powerful Austrasian following
with which he went to war. And the system was continued after his time.

In the 9th century the kings exacted an
oath of vassalage from all the magnates of
the kingdom, and even from the bishops.
It became increasingly apparent that only
those were truly submissive to the king who
had paid homage to him. Thus the subject
was disappearing behind the vassal, and
Hincmar went so far as to warn Charles
the Bald of the consequent danger to the
royal authority. The necessity in which the
first mayors of the palace found themselves,
of providing themselves with loyal troops,
consisting of sworn beneficiaries, led to a
profound transformation of the State. For
henceforth the king would be compelled to
reckon with his vassals, who constituted the
military strength of the State. The organization of the counties fell into disorder,
since the vassals were not amenable to the
jurisdiction of the count. In the field they
commanded their own vassals themselves;
the count led only the freemen to battle. It
is possible that their domains were exempt
from taxation. They were known as *opti-
mates regis.*

The chronicle of Moissac, in 813, called
them *senatus* or *majores natu Francorum,*
and together with the high ecclesiastics and
the counts they did indeed form the king's
council. The king, therefore, allowed them
to partake of his political power. The State
was becoming dependent on the contrac-
tual bonds established between the king
and his vassals.

This was the beginning of the feudal
period.

All might still have been well if the king
could have retained his vassals. But at the
close of the 9th century, apart from those
of his own domain, they had become subject to the suzerainty of the counts. For as
the royal power declined, from the time of
the civil wars which marked the end of the
reign of Louis the Pious, the counts became
more and more independent. The only relation which existed between them and the

king was that of the vassal to his suzerain.
They collected the *regalia* for the king; and
sometimes they combined several counties
into one.[8] The monarchy lost its administrative character, becoming transformed
into a *bloc* of independent principalities,
attached to the king by a bond of vassalage
which he could no longer force his vassals
to respect. The kings allowed the royal
power to slip through their fingers.

And it was inevitable that it should be
so. We must not be misled by the prestige
of Charlemagne. He was still able to rule
the State by virtue of his military power,
his wealth, which was derived from booty,
and his *de facto* pre-eminence in the
Church. These things enabled him to reign
without systematic finances, and to exact
obedience from functionaries who, being
one and all great landowners, could very
well have existed in independence. But
what is the value of an administration
which is no longer salaried? How can it be
prevented from administering the country,
if it chooses, for its own benefit, and not
for the king's? Of what real use were such
inspectors as the *missi?* Charles undoubtedly intended to administer the kingdom,
but was unable to do so. When we read the
capitularies, we are struck by the difference
between what they decreed and what was
actually effected. Charles decreed that
everyone should send his sons to school;
that there should be only one mint; that
usurious prices should be abolished in time
of famine. He established maximum prices.
But it was impossible to realize all these
things, because to do so would have pre-
supposed the obedience — which could not
be assured — of the *grandi,* who were conscious of their independence, or of the
bishops, who, when Charlemagne was
dead, proclaimed the superiority of the
spiritual over the temporal power.

The economic basis of the State did not
correspond with the administrative character which Charlemagne had endeavoured

[8] In this connection the history of the formation
of the county of Flanders is highly characteristic.
[Pirenne's note]

to preserve. The economy of the State was based upon the great domain without commercial outlets.

The landowners had no need of security, since they did not engage in commerce. Such a form of property is perfectly consistent with anarchy. Those who owned the soil had no need of the king.

Was this why Charles had endeavoured to preserve the class of humble freemen? He made the attempt, but he was unsuccessful. The great domain continued to expand, and liberty to disappear.

When the Normans began to invade the country, the State was already powerless. It was incapable of taking systematic measures of defence, and of assembling armies which could have held their own against the invaders. There was no agreement between the defenders. One may say with Hartmann: *Heer und Staat werden durch die Grundherrschaft und das Lehnwesen zersetzt.*

What was left of the king's *regalia* he misused. He relinquished the *tonlieu,* and the right of the mint. Of its own accord the monarchy divested itself of its remaining inheritance, which was little enough. In the end, royalty became no more than a form. Its evolution was completed when in France, with Hugh Capet, it became elective.

INTELLECTUAL CIVILIZATION

As we have seen, the Germanic invasions had not the effect of abolishing Latin as the language of "Romania," except in those territories where Salic and Ripuarian Franks, Alamans, and Bavarians had established themselves *en masse.* Elsewhere the German immigrants became Romanized with surprising rapidity.

The conquerors, dispersed about the country, and married to native wives who continued to speak their own language, all learned the Latin tongue. They did not modify it in any way, apart from introducing a good many terms relating to law, the chase, war, and agriculture, which made their way southwards from the Belgian regions, where the Germans were numerous.

Even more rapid was the Romanization of the Burgundi, Visigoths, Ostrogoths, Vandals and Lombards. According to Gamillscheg, nothing was left of the Gothic language when the Moors conquered Spain but the names of persons and places.

On the other hand, the confusion into which the Mediterranean world was thrown by the invasion of Islam resulted in a profound transformation where language was concerned. In Africa Latin was replaced by Arabic. In Spain, on the other hand, it survived, but was deprived of its foundations: there were no more schools or monasteries, and there was no longer an educated clergy. The conquered people made use of a Roman patois which was not a written language. Latin, which had survived so successfully in the Peninsula until the eve of the conquest, disappeared; people were beginning to speak Spanish.

In Italy, on the other hand, it resisted more successfully; and a few isolated schools survived in Rome and Milan.

But it is in Gaul that we can best observe the extent of the confusion, and its causes.

The Latin of the Merovingian epoch was, of course, barbarously incorrect; but it was still a living Latin. It seems that it was even taught in the schools where a practical education was given, while here and there the bishops and senators still read and sometimes even tried to write the classic Latin.

The Merovingian Latin was by no means a vulgar language. It showed few signs of Germanic influence. Those who spoke it could make themselves understood, and understand others, in any part of "Romania." It was perhaps more incorrect in the North of France than elsewhere, but nevertheless, it was a spoken and written language. The Church did not hesitate to employ it for the purposes of propaganda, administration, and justice.

This language was taught in the schools. Laymen learned and wrote it. Its relation to the Latin of the Empire was like that of the cursive in which it was written to the writing of the Roman epoch. And since it was still written and extensively employed for the purposes of administration and commerce, it became stabilized.

But it was destined to disappear in the course of the great disorders of the 8th century. The political anarchy, the reorganization of the Church, the disappearance of the cities and of commerce and administration, especially the financial administration, and of the secular schools, made its survival, with its Latin soul, impossible. It became debased, and was transformed, according to the region, into various Romanic dialects. The details of the process are lost, but it is certain that Latin ceased to be spoken about the year 800, except by the clergy.

Now, it was precisely at this moment, when Latin ceased to be a living language, and was replaced by the rustic idioms from which the national languages are derived, that it became what it was to remain through the centuries: a learned language: a novel mediaeval feature which dates from the Carolingian epoch.

It is curious to note that the origin of this phenomenon must be sought in the only Romanic country in which the Germanic invasion had completely extirpated Romanism: in Britain, among the Anglo-Saxons.

The conversion of this country was organized, as we have seen, on the shores of the Mediterranean, and not in the neighbouring country of Gaul. It was the monks of Augustine, despatched by Gregory the Great in 596, who promoted the movement already commenced by the Celtic monks of Ireland.

In the 7th century Saint Theodore of Tarsus and his companion Adrian enriched the religion which they brought with them by the Graeco-Roman traditions. A new culture immediately began to evolve in the island, a fact which Dawson rightly considers "the most important event which occurred between the epoch of Justinian and that of Charlemagne." Among these purely Germanic Anglo-Saxons the Latin culture was introduced suddenly, together with

the Latin religion, and it profited by the enthusiasm felt for the latter. No sooner were they converted, under the influence and guidance of Rome, than the Anglo-Saxons turned their gaze toward the Sacred City. They visited it continually, bringing back relics and manuscripts. They submitted themselves to its suggestive influence, and learned its language, which for them was no vulgar tongue, but a sacred language, invested with an incomparable prestige. As early as the 7th century there were men among the Anglo-Saxons, like the Venerable Bede and the poet Aldhelm, whose learning was truly astonishing as measured by the standards of Western Europe.

The intellectual reawakening which took place under Charlemagne must be attributed to the Anglo-Saxon missionaries. Before them, of course, there were the Irish monks, including the greatest of all, Saint Columban, the founder of Luxeuil and Bobbio, who landed in Gaul about 590. They preached asceticism in a time of religious decadence, but we do not find that they exercised the slightest literary influence.

It was quite otherwise with the Anglo-Saxons; their purpose was to propagate Christianity in Germany, a country for which the Merovingian Church had done little or nothing. And this purpose coincided with the policy of the Carolingians; hence the enormous influence of Boniface, the organizer of the Germanic Church, and, by virtue of this fact, the intermediary between the Pope and Pippin the Short.

Charlemagne devoted himself to the task of literary revival simultaneously with that of the restoration of the Church. The principal representative of Anglo-Saxon culture, Alcuin, the head of the school of York, entered Charlemagne's service in 782, as director of the palace school, and henceforth exercised a decisive influence over the literary movement of the time.

Thus, by the most curious reversal of affairs, which affords the most striking proof of the rupture effected by Islam, the North in Europe replaced the South both as a literary and as a political centre.

It was the North that now proceeded to diffuse the culture which it had received from the Mediterranean. Latin, which had been a living language on the further side of the Channel, was for the Anglo-Saxons, from the beginning, merely the language of the Church. The Latin which was taught to the Anglo-Saxons was not the incorrect business and administrative language, adapted to the needs of secular life, but the language which was still spoken in the Mediterranean schools. Theodore came from Tarsus in Cilicia, and had studied at Athens before coming to Rome. Adrian, an African by birth, was the abbot of a monastery near Naples, and was equally learned in Greek and in Latin.

It was the classic tradition that they propagated among their neophytes, and a correct Latin, which had no need, as on the continent, to make concessions to common usage in order to be understood, since the people did not speak Latin, but Anglo-Saxon. Thus, the English monasteries received the heritage of the ancient culture without intermediary. It was the same in the 15th century, when the Byzantine scholars brought to Italy, not the vulgar Greek, the living language of the street, but the classical Greek of the schools.

In this way the Anglo-Saxons became simultaneously the reformers of the language and also the reformers of the Church. The barbarism into which the Church had lapsed was manifested at once by its bad morals, its bad Latin, its bad singing, and its bad writing. To reform it at all meant to reform all these things. Hence questions of grammar and of writing immediately assumed all the significance of an apostolate. Purity of dogma and purity of language went together. Like the Anglo-Saxons, who had immediately adopted it, the Roman rite made its way into all parts of the Empire, together with the Latin culture. This latter was the instrument *par excellence* of what is known as the Carolingian Renaissance, although

this had other agents in such men as Paulus Diaconus, Peter of Pisa, and Theodulf.[9] But it is important to note that this Renaissance was purely clerical. It did not affect the people, who had no understanding of it. It was at once a revival of the antique tradition and a break with the Roman tradition, which was interrupted by the seizure of the Mediterranean regions by Islam. The lay society of the period, being purely agricultural and military, no longer made use of Latin. This was now merely the language of the priestly caste, which monopolized all learning, and which was constantly becoming more divorced from the people whose divinely appointed guide it considered itself. For centuries there had been no learning save in the Church. The consequence was that learning and intellectual culture, while they became more assertive, were also becoming more exceptional. The Carolingian Renaissance coincided with the general illiteracy of the laity. Under the Merovingians laymen were still able to read and write; but not so under the Carolingians. The sovereign who instigated and supported this movement, Charlemagne, could not write; nor could his father, Pippin the Short. We must not attach any real importance to his ineffectual attempts to bestow this culture upon his court and his family. To please him, a few courtiers learnt Latin. Men like Eginhard, Nithard and Angilbert[10] were passing luminaries. Generally speaking, the immense majority of the lay aristocracy were unaffected by a movement which interested

[9] Paulus Diaconus (Paul the Deacon) wrote the very important *History of the Lombards;* Peter of Pisa was a grammarian first at Pavia and then at the Palace School at Aachen; Theodulf was a Spanish Goth who became Bishop of Orléans and is recognized as the best poet of the "Carolingian Renaissance." All were contemporaries of Charlemagne. [Editor's note]

[10] Angilbert, d. 814, was a poet and probably one of the authors of the "Royal Annals" of Charlemagne's period, drawn up in the monastery at Lorsch. Nithard was a son of Angilbert and a grandson of Charlemagne, who wrote several histories of the first half of the ninth century; these contain the famous Oath of Strasbourg (842) in both French and German. [Editor's note]

only those of its members who wished to make a career in the Church.

In the Merovingian epoch the royal administration called for a certain culture on the part of those laymen who wished to enter it. But now, in so far as it still required literate recruits — as it did, for example, for the chancellery — it obtained them from the Church. For the rest, since it no longer had a bureaucracy, it had no further need of men of education. The immense majority of the counts were no doubt illiterate. The type of the Merovingian senator had disappeared. The aristocracy no longer spoke Latin, and apart from a very few exceptions, which prove the rule, it could neither read nor write.

A final characteristic of the Carolingian Renaissance was the reformed handwriting which was introduced at this period. This reform consisted in the substitution of the minuscule for the cursive script: that is to say, a deliberate calligraphy for a current hand. As long as the Roman tradition survived, the Roman cursive was written by all the peoples of the Mediterranean basin. It was, in a certain sense, a business hand, or, at all events, the writing of a period when writing was an everyday necessity. And the diffusion of papyrus was simultaneous with this constant need of corresponding and recording. The great crisis of the 8th century inevitably restricted the practice of writing. It was hardly required any longer except for making copies of books. Now, for this purpose the majuscule and the uncial were employed. These scripts were introduced into Ireland when the country was converted to Christianity. And in Ireland, not later than the close of the 7th century, the uncial (semi-uncial) gave rise to the minuscule, which was already employed in the antiphonary of Bangor (680–690). The Anglo-Saxons took these manuscripts, together with those which were brought by the missionaries deriving from Rome, as their example and pattern. It was from the insular minuscule and the Roman *scriptoria,* in which the semi-uncial was much employed, that the

perfected or Caroline minuscule was derived at the beginning of the 9th century.

The first dated example of this minuscule is found in the evangelary written by Godescalc in 781, at the request of Charlemagne, who was himself unable to write. Alcuin made the monastery of Tours a centre of diffusion for this new writing, which was to determine the whole subsequent graphological evolution of the Middle Ages.

A number of monasteries, which might be compared to the printing-offices of the Renaissance, provided for the increasing demand for books and the diffusion of these new characters. In addition to Tours, there were Corbie, Orleans, Saint Denis, Saint Wandrille, Fulda, Corvey, Saint Gall, Reichenau, and Lorsch. In most of them, and above all in Fulda, there were Anglo-Saxon monks. It will be noted that nearly all these monasteries were situated in the North, between the Seine and the Weser. It was in this region, of which the original Carolingian domains formed the centre, that the new ecclesiastical culture, or, shall we say, the Carolingian Renaissance, attained its greatest efflorescence.

Thus we observe the same phenomenon in every domain of life. The culture which had hitherto flourished in the Mediterranean countries had migrated to the North. It was in the North that the civilization of the Middle Ages was elaborated. And it is a striking fact that the majority of the writers of this period were of Irish, Anglo-Saxon or Frankish origin: that is, they came from regions which lay to the north of the Seine. . . .

Thus we see that Germany, being converted, immediately began to play an essential part in the civilization to which she had hitherto been a stranger. The culture which had been entirely Roman was now becoming Romano-Germanic, but if truth be told it was localized in the bosom of the Church.

Nevertheless, it is evident that a new orientation was unconsciously effected in Europe, and that in this development Germanism collaborated. Charlemagne's court, and Charlemagne himself, were certainly much less Latinized than were the Merovingians. Under the new dispensation many functionaries were recruited from Germany, and Austrasian vassals were settled in the South. Charlemagne's wives were all German women. Certain judicial reforms, such as that of the sheriffs, had their origin in the regions which gave birth to the dynasty. Under Pippin the clergy became Germanized and under Charlemagne there were many German bishops in Romanic regions. Angelelmus and Heribald, at Auxerre, were both Bavarians; Bernold, at Strasbourg, was a Saxon; at Mans there were three Westphalians in succession; Hilduin, at Verdun, was a German; Herulfus and Ariolfus, at Langres, came from Augsburg; Wulferius, at Vienne, and Leidrad, at Lyons, were Bavarians. And I do not think there is any evidence of a contrary migration. To appreciate the difference we have only to compare Chilperic,[11] a Latin poet, with Charlemagne, at whose instance a collection was made of the ancient Germanic songs!

All this was bound to result in a break with the Roman and Mediterranean traditions. And while it made the West more and more self-sufficing, it produced an aristocracy of mixed descent and inheritance. Was it not then that many terms found

[11] Chilperic was King of the Franks, 561–584. [Editor's note]

their way into the vocabulary to which an earlier origin has often been attributed? There were no longer any Barbarians. There was one great Christian community, coterminous with the *ecclesia*. This *ecclesia*, of course, looked toward Rome, but Rome had broken away from Byzantium and was bound to look toward the North. The Occident was now living its own life. It was preparing to unfold its possibilities, its virtualities, taking no orders from the outer world, except in the matter of religion.

There was now a community of civilization, of which the Carolingian Empire was the symbol and the instrument. For while the Germanic element collaborated in this civilization, it was a Germanic element which had been Romanized by the Church. There were, of course, differences within this community. The Empire would be dismembered, but each of its portions would survive, since the feudality would respect the monarchy. In short, the culture which was to be that of the period extending from the early Middle Ages to the Renaissance of the 12th century — and this was a true renaissance — bore, and would continue to bear, the Carolingian imprint. There was an end of political unity, but an international unity of culture survived. Just as the States founded in the West in the 5th century by the Barbarian kings retained the Roman imprint, so France, Germany, and Italy retained the Carolingian imprint.

GENERAL CONCLUSION

From the foregoing data, it seems, we may draw two essential conclusions:

1. The Germanic invasions destroyed neither the Mediterranean unity of the ancient world, nor what may be regarded as the truly essential features of the Roman culture as it still existed in the 5th century, at a time when there was no longer an Emperor in the West.

Despite the resulting turmoil and destruction, no new principles made their appearance; neither in the economic or social order, nor in the linguistic situation, nor in the existing institutions. What civilization survived was Mediterranean. It was in the regions by the sea that culture was preserved, and it was from them that the innovations of the age proceeded: monasticism, the conversion of the Anglo-Saxons, the *ars Barbarica*, etc.

The Orient was the fertilizing factor: Constantinople, the centre of the world. In

600 the physiognomy of the world was not different in quality from that which it had revealed in 400.

2. The cause of the break with the tradition of antiquity was the rapid and unexpected advance of Islam. The result of this advance was the final separation of East from West, and the end of the Mediterranean unity. Countries like Africa and Spain, which had always been parts of the Western community, gravitated henceforth in the orbit of Baghdad. In these countries another religion made its appearance, and an entirely different culture. The Western Mediterranean, having become a Musulman lake, was no longer the thoroughfare of commerce and of thought which it had always been.

The West was blockaded and forced to live upon its own resources. For the first time in history the axis of life was shifted northwards from the Mediterranean. The decadence into which the Merovingian monarchy lapsed as a result of this change gave birth to a new dynasty, the Carolingian, whose original home was in the Germanic North.

With this new dynasty the Pope allied himself, breaking with the Emperor, who, engrossed in his struggle against the Musulmans, could no longer protect him. And so the Church allied itself with the new order of things. In Rome, and in the Empire which it founded, it had no rival. And its power was all the greater inasmuch as the State, being incapable of maintaining its administration, allowed itself to be absorbed by the feudality, the inevitable sequel of the economic regression. All the consequences of this change became glaringly apparent after Charlemagne. Europe, dominated by the Church and the feudality, assumed a new physiognomy, differing slightly in different regions. The Middle Ages — to retain the traditional term — were beginning. The transitional phase was protracted. One may say that it lasted a whole century — from 650 to 750. It was during this period of anarchy that the tradition of antiquity disappeared, while the new elements came to the surface.

This development was completed in 800 by the constitution of the new Empire, which consecrated the break between the West and the East, inasmuch as it gave to the West a new Roman Empire — the manifest proof that it had broken with the old Empire, which continued to exist in Constantinople.

ORIGINS OF MEDIEVAL CIVILIZATION AND THE PROBLEM OF CONTINUITY

J. LESTOCQUOY

Jean François Lestocquoy (1903–   ), a French medievalist, has been associated since 1931 with the institution of Saint-Joseph of Arras and has been active in various historical societies of the department of Pas-de-Calais. Lestocquoy is now recognized as the chief authority on the history of this region, which, in the early Middle Ages, became a possession of the Count of Flanders and then, as now, had special importance by reason of its strategic situation near the English Channel.

I

THE BIRTH of a civilization, the changes in ideas and outward forms, maybe in the very appearance of the country, which such an event involves, must always be of the deepest interest to historians. Hence the general preoccupation with that obscure period, which, for good or ill, has been termed the Dark Ages. Where are the origins of medieval civilization to be found? The theory that first held the field looked for its answers to Rome: certain elements of Roman civilization had always survived, particularly in the organization of the towns. Then there was a reaction, and the Roman theory was rejected, in a manner perhaps too sweeping. With the single reservation that in Italy alone some memories of Roman civilization might have survived, all was attributed to the Germans, the true founders of medieval civilization.

Both theories are open to the same criticism, that they view the problem too exclusively from the juridical point of view. Life is not so simple as lawyers would make it, and juridical concepts alone cannot provide an explanation of medieval civilization. Neither Rome nor the barabarians are

enough; the origins of medieval civilization are to be sought in the development of the peoples themselves.

The view which is at present the most widely accepted is that of Henri Pirenne. According to him, medieval civilization began to take shape at the end of the tenth century after the Viking and Hungarian invasions had ceased. The end of the ancient world had come much earlier. The triumph of Islam shattered the unity of the Mediterranean and severed those relations with the east and with ancient civilization which had still been maintained under the Merovingians. There had then been a sudden breach with the past, and the Carolingian period was one of full decline. Charlemagne was thrown back on the resources of northern Europe, and life became self-centred as never before. Civilization became completely rural, with the great domain as its normal expression. Towns, or at least towns worthy of the name, no longer existed, and merchants sank to the level of common pedlars. This retrogression of economic life was accentuated by the Viking invasions. Only at the

From J. Lestocquoy, "The Tenth Century," *The Economic History Review*, XVII (No. 1, 1947), pp. 1–6. By permission of the author and *The Economic History Review*.

very end of the tenth century did Europe begin to revive, and then under influences coming from the east by way of Venice. A merchant class came into being and gave importance to the towns, gradually replacing the pedlars and Jews who for three centuries had maintained such little commerce as had continued to exist. At first these merchants were wanderers without any permanent home, adventurers thrown up by the surplus population of the countryside. It was only gradually that they settled down. Towns came into existence in spots favoured by nature, either at natural harbours or at points inland where rivers ceased to be navigable. In these settlements merchants were all-important and were able to create for themselves their own law, the *jus mercatorum*.

The theory is attractive enough, and the last part of it at least has been generally admitted. But the first part has been widely questioned. Many historians have refused to admit that the growth of Islam was so decisive a factor in the development of Europe. The studies of M. Sabbe on the commerce in precious stuffs appeared to show that the Mediterranean trade was interrupted less completely than Pirenne had thought. It was even possible to argue that the Carolingian period saw an advance in commerce and not a decline. F. L. Ganshof showed that there was still some commerce in the ports of Provence between the eighth and the tenth centuries.[1] R. S. Lopez, looking at the question from the point of view of the east, sought to explain the decline by the weakening of the relations with Constantinople: a process which was chronologically independent of the expansion of Islam.

Would it not therefore be right to admit that although the career of Mohammed must have had a considerable influence on developments in Europe it was less decisive and less easy to define than Pirenne believed? Nor was there a sharp contrast

[1] Sabbe and Ganshof are Belgian historians. [Editor's note]

between the Merovingian and Carolingian periods. In the ninth century there must have been still professional merchants and a certain amount of commerce. In the northern regions of the Frankish empire economic life may even have continued to progress when the invasions, Norman first and Hungarian afterwards, took place.

With the invasions the problem of continuity comes up again. Was there really a sharp break between the period preceding the invasions and that which followed them? Must one regard the development of towns in the eleventh century as a kind of spontaneous generation? For such is in fact the theory of Pirenne. For him the towns were something entirely new; their inhabitants were adventurers coming from places unknown, a surplus population of a countryside which was increasing in numbers at a prodigious rate. Thus from a class of ruthless men there sprang that merchant class, which was in time to give birth to the urban patriciate and to impart to the towns of the Middle Ages their peculiar character.

II

These questions could only be answered by a more elaborate study of tenth-century conditions than is possible in this short essay. Such a study would have to include not only Flanders, where documentary evidence, save for the south, is very scanty, but also Germany and Italy. For there is still another question that one must ask, and that is, whether the development of these regions was independent or interconnected? Were their towns and merchants unique specimens, or did they form part of a western whole? My own feeling is that these regions were only at slightly different stages of development, and that the less fortunate of the newest regions, such as Flanders, were constantly tending to catch up with the social development of those regions which were more advanced. One has the impression that the government of towns by the *bourgeoisie* was a kind of norm in the Middle Ages. It was the goal to which everything was tending, although the point of departure in different regions might not always be the same.

The lines of demarcation between region and region were never sharp. Above all, the merchant *bourgeoisie,* without being vagrant, was extremely well-travelled and far from ignorant about affairs of other countries, however distant. Guilland, in his lectures at the Sorbonne in 1940, called attention to the remarkable similarities between the organization of the silk industry at Constantinople and that of the cloth industry at Florence and Douai in the tenth and eleventh centuries, and that of England in the later centuries. This influence must have been disseminated by the famous *Livre du Préfet.* In the realm of art the eastern derivation of Romanesque is generally admitted; why should similar influences have been absent from the field of ideas and social organization?

The literature on the origins of our civilization will reveal to what a surprising extent the fog of silence envelops the tenth century. It almost seems as if we must renounce all hope of ever knowing all that happened during that period. Apart from a few illuminated manuscripts, it has left little behind in the way of works of art, and this lacuna is the more significant in view of the brilliant achievements of the Carolingian period and the amazing triumphs of the eleventh century, "le siècle des grandes expériences," as Focillon[2] has called it. Nor did this period produce anything of importance in the way of literature. Its most valuable writer was Flodoard: what could we have done without him? Yet for him, as for most of his contemporaries, annals and history were interchangeable terms. He lines up his facts in the most precise fashion, so to speak, end to end, without bothering about their interrelations. Compared to Einhard in the ninth century and Raoul Glaber in the eleventh century, Flodoard

is not a historian.[3] Einhard and Raoul Glaber do not merely relate the succession of events; they give form to their material and try to interpret it, they give us their own views, in short. Flodoard, on the other hand, describes a mere succession of independent events. His precision is something we must be grateful for; but his want of ideas betrays the decadence of his age.

At the same time the production of annals was entirely suited to the period. Men were compelled to live in the present, as Lot has observed.[4] The students of the history of the early Middle Ages, and of the tenth century in particular, will be struck by the total absence of political ideas, of clear-cut intellectual schemes, of all notion of continuity. We cannot attribute political or economic aims to the rulers of the period without committing a grave anachronism. In the sparsely populated regions of the north, the only object of policy seems to have been that of territorial conquest, which is surely not a sign of mature political thought. To a historian in search of political ideas or economic policies, nothing can be more disconcerting than the general history of the period: a mere record of petty personal rivalries. France was a prey to constant civil war, and although Count Arnulf succeeded in building up a strong power in Flanders in the middle of the tenth century, his death was followed by a relapse into anarchy. Germany under the Saxon emperors alone gives the impression of any real political organization.

Why this should have been so is easy to understand, for the state of insecurity prevailed over the greater part of Europe. One is tempted to forget how long the scourge

2 Henri Focillon, French historian, was the author of an important book, *L'an mil (The Year One Thousand),* Paris, 1952. [Editor's note]

3 Einhard (ca. 770–840) was associated with the palace school at Aachen and was the author of a celebrated *Life of Charlemagne.* Raoul Glaber (ca. 1000–1050) was a Benedictine chronicler at St. Germain d'Auxerre and wrote a kind of history of the world, from 900 to 1045. Flodoard (10th century) wrote a history of the church of Rheims, valuable mainly for the documents included. [Editor's note]

4 Ferdinand Lot, *Les derniers carolingiens* (Paris, 1891), p. 168.

of the invasions continued, and to assume that those of the Northmen ceased in 883 and were followed by a period of peace. But, if we merely turn over the pages of Flodoard, we can easily see what an illusion this is. The Normans occupied Brittany in 921. The Hungarians devastated Italy in 922 and sacked Pavia, one of the most important towns in Europe, in 924. During the same years the Normans continued their devastations in Aquitaine and Auvergne. In 925 they invaded the valley of the Somme and advanced as far as Noyon. In the single year 926, King Robert of France defeated the Normans at Fauquembergue in Artois, there was a Norman invasion of the valley of Loire, and there were two Hungarian invasions. The very rumour of the approach of the Hungarians was sufficient to cause a general flight of the country-folk with their relics to the shelter of the towns. The terrible raids of the Hungarians were continued in 933 and 935, and on a vaster scale in 955. In Italy after a devastation by Berengar in 962 somewhat more peaceful conditions returned, but even then the peace was only a comparative one. Bands of Saracens watched over the Alpine passes, where until 973 or 983 they blocked the route and killed travellers or held them to ransom, thus impeding communications between Italy and the rest of Europe. How could trade survive under such conditions? More especially, how could it proceed in lands where Norman raids appear to have reduced the towns to petty insignificance?

Besides the circumstances, the men themselves must be taken into account. We know that the economy of the period was mainly rural, but unfortunately we know almost nothing about the rural life of the period. This is the more unfortunate since the intense local urban life, which characterized the later Middle Ages and lasted until the appearance of powerful and centralized states with capital cities had reduced other towns to positions of secondary importance, was not yet born. In the tenth century the countryside and the manor took precedence over the towns — a circumstance which differentiates most sharply the west from the east.

There is, however, one characteristic of the period that must be emphasized, for it is not always immediately apparent in the texts, and only becomes apparent if viewed in the perspective of centuries. This is the remarkable weakness, the minute scale, of all things. Let us take for example the towns and military operations as measured by the scale of the fortified places. We find that Montreuil-sur-Mer (which recent studies have shown to have had an unexpected importance in the Middle Ages) was constantly an object of dispute between Flanders and Normandy. But the fragments of the town wall, now surviving in private gardens, can still be seen, and its towers are so small that they make one think of children's games rather than of military operations. Similarly, Senlis successfully resisted capture by Louis d'Outremer and Otto I in 946, and the texts refer to the strength of its walls. . . . But these were Roman walls which had already existed for six centuries. Amiens had also retained its Roman walls. When in 950, Arnulf of Flanders was at war with Herbert of Vermandois, the latter took possession of a tower already occupied by the Bishop of Amiens, so that each of the two belligerents was installed in a tower, each serving as a diminutive fortress. There is something almost comic about a war on this scale. Laon, which was captured in 949 only by a stratagem, was scarcely more redoubtable.

All this indicates that the armies were feeble, the towns petty; certainly a place of several thousand inhabitants would take rank as a great city. And even so, great towns of this kind were mostly to be found north of the Seine, in that part of France which still retained some vitality. What do we know of the future great cities of the Middle Ages; of Florence, Siena, Pisa and Lucca? These were all little townships, too small to be mentioned. The same is true of Ghent and St-Omer; the silence of our authorities is not pure accident. Almost the only places mentioned in those regions which were to be the scene of intense economic activity in the eleventh century are Rheims, Arras and Verdun in France, and Pavia, Milan and Venice in Italy.

Indeed it is possible to develop this theme further and to argue that urban life in the west had been reduced to the minimum. This has in fact often been done, and Pirenne makes it one of the main bases of his argument. Whatever view we take, it is certain that in this respect the west was sharply differentiated from the east. The west has nothing comparable to a city like Constantinople. We need not perhaps give credence to the tale that Constantinople had a population of a million and Thessalonica of five hundred thousand, but there can be no doubt that the cities were on a scale no longer known in Europe. . . .

ECONOMIC CONSEQUENCES OF THE
BARBARIAN INVASIONS

H. ST. L. B. MOSS

Henry St. Lawrence Beaufort Moss has been associated in historical
writing with Professor Norman H. Baynes. In Britain they have greatly
opened up the study of Byzantine history. Among Mr. Moss' publications
is an excellent text, *The Birth of the Middle Ages, 395–814.* The selection
which follows reprints in its entirety an article by Mr. Moss in a series on
"Revisions in Economic History," in the British journal, *The Economic
History Review.* Mr. Moss wrote this article in 1937 as a summary of
historical investigation at that time. For his extensive documentation the
student is referred to the original article.

DURING the past generation a substantial literature has accumulated
round one of the central problems of
European history — the transition from the
ancient world to medieval civilisation. By
the end of the nineteenth century what
may be called the "catastrophic" view had
been definitely abandoned. Since then the
complexity of the change has become
steadily more apparent. How distant any
general agreement still is, even on its main
features, was shown by the debates of the
Historical Congress at Oslo in 1928; and
detailed re-examination of its many aspects
proceeds unceasingly in a score of periodicals and a steady flow of monographs. A
cursory and superficial survey of some of
the principal points of controversy is all
that will be attempted in the following
pages.

The economic approach to history is a
comparatively recent development. Ancient
and medieval writers were seldom directly
concerned with the subject, and not till the
last century did it emerge as a definite
subdivision of historiography. A revaluation
of many historical judgments followed,
based on a fresh sifting of the sources.
But an important obstacle to the new
studies, so far as the "dark ages" are concerned, soon made its appearance. Deficient
in general as the sources for these centuries
are, nowhere is their poverty more thread-
bare than in the economic data which they
provide. Scanty references, often of purely
local application, in the writings of annal-
ists, orators, monkish chroniclers or theologians must be collected, interpreted, and
assessed in the light of a background which
is often only too obscure, before any general
picture can be formed. Population statistics,
estimates of money-values, even, in many
cases, identification of place-names — these,
and much else, are highly problematical.
Epigraphic and archaeological evidence is
notably insufficient, as compared with that
of the preceding centuries. It is no disserv-
ice to the results achieved by recent scholarship to point out that the material at its
disposal is lamentably small in proportion

From H. St. L. B. Moss, "The Economic Consequences of the Barbarian Invasions," *The Economic
History Review,* VII (May, 1937), 209–216. Published for The Economic History Society by A. & C.
Black, Ltd., London. Reprinted by permission of the Economic History Society and Mr. Moss.

to the difficulty and extent of the problem. This being so, it is arguable that comprehensive theories should be regarded at present rather as working hypotheses to be tested and possibly modified by gradually accumulating data, than as definite solutions to which all such data must necessarily conform.

"Barbarian Invasions" is a wide term, covering more than a millennium. For our present purpose we may define it as the Germanic settlements which, during the fifth and sixth centuries A.D., led to the breakdown of Roman government in the western provinces. This will exclude such later developments as the Slavs, the Northmen, the Magyars, and (except incidentally) the Arabs. The eastern Mediterranean, where Roman administration continued to operate, is also excluded, though it was undoubtedly, during the whole of this period, the commercial focus of Europe. Spain and Africa, owing to the Islamic conquests, stand apart; and evidence concerning them is in any case insufficient for any brief generalisations. Britain is also, at this time, removed from the main course of western European history, and its special problems will not be entered upon here.

The economic significance of the invasions has been presented in a fresh light by the results of recent investigation, which has led to a general softening down of climaxes and contrasts. *Kulturcäsur*, an abrupt break of cultural continuity, is no longer in question: for Rostovtzeff "what happened was a slow and gradual change, a shifting of values in the consciousness of men," though he admits the virtual disappearance of the Graeco-Roman city organisation, and a reduction of ancient civilisation to some essential elements. Chronologically, he adds, this "coincides with the political disintegration of the Roman Empire, and with a great change in its social and economic life." This simplification of the complex structure of the ancient world can be traced from the unsettled conditions which succeeded the Antonine Age, at the close of the second

century; it is from this period, in F. Lot's view,[1] that the Middle Ages should properly be dated. The pace of regression was therefore slow; and the continued contact and gradual fusion of the Roman and Germanic worlds, which was made possible by the survival, until the opening of the fifth century, of the Roman Empire in the West — thanks largely to the measures of Diocletian and Constantine — enabled many Roman institutions to pass into the structure of the barbarian kingdoms.

The details of this fusion have received much attention. Early German settlements within the frontiers have been noticed; the careers of Germans in Roman service have been traced. Economic and cultural relations between the Empire and the barbarians have been studied. . . . The agrarian systems of the later Roman Empire and of the Teutonic peoples have given rise to much controversial literature. The contrast formerly drawn between the free association of the "Mark" of primitive German agriculture and the despotic control of the great Roman estates had been abandoned, or seriously modified, by the end of last century, and emphasis is now laid by certain writers on the inequalities of German social classes and the essential continuity in landholding arrangements, from the ancient to the medieval worlds. Thus H. Sée, developing the teaching of Fustel de Coulanges, claims that in France "le personnel des propriétaires pourra changer au cours des temps, mais la villa et le manse subsisteront pendant des siècles, souvent avec leur dimensions primitives."[2] Italian authorities have similarly dwelt on the Roman survivals in their

---

[1] This view was developed by Ferdinand Lot in his *The End of the Ancient World and the Beginnings of the Middle Ages*, London, 1931. [Editor's note]

[2] "the personnel of the owners will change in time, but the villa and the 'manse' will persist for centuries, often with their original boundaries." Henri Sée (1864–1930) was a leading French economic historian. Fustel de Coulanges (1830–1889) developed a theory of Roman origins of feudalism, which though not generally accepted had a significant influence on historical interpretations in his day. [Editor's note]

country, not only in the organisation of the great estates, but in the city-centered life of the Lombards, and, as has been suggested, in the continued existence, even so late as the tenth century, of "artisan corporations" akin to those which characterised the industrial system of the later Roman state.

Examination of the conditions prevailing in the Romano-German kingdoms has shown a compromise rather than a conquest, varying in the degree with the different peoples, but — such is the trend of much recent theory — with a considerably larger admixture of Roman elements that was formerly believed. Legal codes, marriage customs and social divisions exhibit many examples of interaction and even, perhaps, convergence of similar institutions, while the role played by the Church in the preservation of Roman legal and juridical methods has lately been brought into full prominence. Nor has the view of an unbroken economic regression, a steady drift towards "natural economy" from the third century onwards, been left unchallenged. It had already been noticed that the currency reforms of Constantine I were followed by a return to the monetary conditions of the earlier Empire, and G. Mickwitz has shown that these continued to exist throughout the fourth century; even the State itself, in whose interests it was to maintain the payments in kind stabilised by Diocletian, had finally to capitulate before the demands of the army and civil service. The Ostrogothic kingdom in Italy, as Hartmann[3] had proved, was still organised on a money basis, the details of which have recently been elucidated by H. Geiss, and Italian writers have even maintained that no real breach is observable between the financial arrangements of the later Roman Empire and those of the Lombard government. Stress, in fact, is in general laid on the prevalence of a "money economy" throughout these centuries, and the denial of any decisive economic change caused by the barbarians has involved the theory that commerce and finance suffered no serious setback.

Two celebrated theories must be mentioned in this connection, those of H. Pirenne and A. Dopsch, though space forbids more than a brief description. In Pirenne's view,[4] the economic organisation of the provinces where the Germans settled underwent no appreciable change. The Mediterranean unity of the ancient world continued unbroken until the Islamic conquests. Merovingian Gaul, in this respect, presented no contrasts with Roman Gaul. During the most flourishing period of Roman rule, Belgium had been in close contact with the Mediterranean world, importing, for instance, for her villas marble from Illyria and Africa and *objets d'art* of Italian or Oriental origin, and exporting hams and geese to the Imperial capital, and pottery and woollen cloaks over the Alpine roads to Italy. "In spite of the scanty evidence, we know for certain that up to about the year 700, Mediterranean commerce was still spreading all kinds of Oriental spices over the country. Papyrus, imported from Egypt, was so plentiful that it could be regularly bought at the market of Cambrai, and no doubt in many other places." In little more than a generation, all this was changed. At the beginning of the Carolingian period, the advance of Islam closed up the Mediterranean along the coast of Gaul, and severed Gallic relations with Syria and Egypt, drying up the stream of commerce from Marseilles. Under these conditions, an economy of regression, of decadence, rapidly set in. The result was the extinction of commerce, industry, and urban life, the disappearance of the merchant class, and the substitution for the "exchange economy" which had previously functioned of an economy occupied solely with the cultivation of the soil and the consumption of its products by the owners. Even Italy and

[3] Ludo M. Hartmann (1865–1924), a German historian who applied the evolutionary approach to the problem of the transition from Rome to Europe. Other historians mentioned in this paragraph are more recent writers. [Editor's note]

[4] The remainder of this paragraph is a summary of Pirenne's views with quotations from his writings. [Editor's note]

the Netherlands, though at first presenting "a striking contrast with the essentially agricultural civilisation to which the closing of the Mediterranean had reduced western Europe," were finally forced to adopt this retrogressive economy, in which payments were largely rendered in kind. A species of *Kulturcäsur* accompanied these developments in France. The Roman lay schools had existed in Merovingian times, and merchants must have been literate to handle the complicated transactions of Mediterranean trade. Commercial culture, however, disappeared in the course of the eighth century; credit and contracts were no longer in use; writing was no longer needed, tallies or chalk marks sufficing for the deals of the local market, and the "mercator" of the ninth-century sources is no longer an educated man of affairs, but a peasant carrying eggs and vegetables once a week to the neighbouring township.

To summarise briefly the work of Dopsch is an even more hazardous task in view of the wide range of his theories and the considerable development which they have undergone. Covering the whole field of economic life from Caesar to Charlemagne, Dopsch has surveyed in detail the evidence for the relations between the German and Roman worlds, the importance of which had been first brought into full prominence in O. Seeck's brilliant work.[5] Emphasis is laid on the recent findings of archaeology, especially in the districts of the Rhine and upper Danube, as showing continuity on the occupied sites, and on the smallness of the difference in cultural level which, it is claimed, separated the German from the Roman population at the time of the invasions. It is no longer possible to regard the German as a mere peasant, or a follower of nomad raiding chiefs; he was also a settled farmer, a seafarer, a skilled merchant, even a city-dweller. The general conclusion, which resembles that of Seeck, is reached that the German peoples pervaded the

Roman Empire from within, by a kind of peaceful penetration; with the coming of the German kingdoms, the old-established firm, as it were, changed its name to that of the long predominant partner. The continuity is worked out in great detail; landholding, social classes, political organization are traced in the various kingdoms up to the time of the Carolingian ascendancy in western Europe. Industry and commerce are likewise held to show no hiatus, save for the temporary disturbances caused by the invasions. Trade still circulated along the Roman roads, carrying not only the luxuries, but the necessities of life. The nobility may have retreated to their country estates, but they remained in contact with the towns (which continued for the most part to exist) and produced for the local market. The whole theory of a regression to "natural economy" and the doctrine of a "closed domestic economy" must therefore be abandoned. The Germans had for centuries been accustomed to the handling of money, and even in the invasion period had carried on extensive trading activities. The Germanic kingdoms were therefore conducted on a currency basis, and financial policy formed part of their political programmes. The Carolingian period, far from showing a decline, as in Pirenne's view, witnessed a considerable extension of trade and industry, and even the dissolution of Charlemagne's Empire was not followed by any regression to autarchic conditions. "The Carolingian development is a link in the unbroken chain of living continuity which leads, without any cultural break, from the late antiquity to the German middle ages."

What, it may be asked, has become of "the great change in social and economic life" to which Rostovtzeff refers? From the studies which we have been analyzing, it would seem that nothing of the sort took place, and that the early Middle Ages preserved intact the fabric of later Roman economic organization. Some reservations may be suggested as regards the theories outlined above. In the first place, none of the attempts to provide a general economic

[5] Otto Seeck (1850–1921) wrote an important six-volume work on the period from Diocletian to 476. [Editor's note]

"pattern" for these centuries has succeeded in establishing itself beyond the reach of controversy. M. Weber and others had pointed to the recession to conditions of "natural Economy" which took place in the third century A. D., and to the settlement of nobles on country estates which supplied all their own needs. . . . Trade was only thinly spread, and the requirements of the State were not met, on the whole by monetary means. K. Bücher, building on this position, then formed his theory of stages, in which three main phases of development were traced in the economic history of Europe. The first, most primitive, stage, that of a "closed house-economy," covered the whole ancient world, and persisted until the tenth century A. D. His view was based, as regards ancient history, on an incomplete analysis, which examined principally the early Greek and late Roman periods. Subsequent work by Beloch and Ed. Meyer, among others, invalidated his conclusions. It was shown that the economic life of the ancient world, especially in the Hellenistic and Roman periods, attained a complexity of organisation which was not reached again till many centuries had passed. These views have been reinforced by epigraphic and archaeological research, and especially by the papyrus evidence from Egypt. Thus the theory of Bücher, as regards the Graeco-Roman world, has long ceased to find any general acceptance. Dopsch, however, complains that its influence continues to dominate the outlook of historical students upon the period under discussion.[6]

Yet the character of the later Roman organisation precludes any unhesitating acceptance in their entirety of Dopsch's views. Perhaps the greatest administrative change in European history was the replacement of the *polis* system by the Roman world-empire. The organism of the self-governing city-state gave way to the new bureaucracy, supporting and supported by the central Imperial power, whose origin lay not in the old *polis* world, but rather in the great "private economies" of the Hellenistic rulers. In the final stage, the constitution of Diocletian and Constantine, the bureaucracy became the executive of the absolutist central government in all branches of administration. Society adapted itself to the new conditions, and the great landowners gained a large measure of control over their dependents. Trade and industry, as Rostovtzeff has shown, were progressively subordinated to the public services. . . . But whereas in the east the centralizing bureaucracy prevailed, in the west, through the weakness, and final breakdown, of the imperial government, it was the decentralising landowners who gained the upper hand. Indeed, in western Europe the decline may have set in long before; but the immense contrast, which recent studies have not weakened, between the east Roman world — with its highly developed administration and civil service, its complex, and largely State-controlled, organisation of trade and commerce — and the chaotic conditions, localised governments and decline of cultural standards in western Europe indicates more surely than anything else the changes wrought by the barbarian invasions.

The onus of proof, therefore, lies on those who would seek to show that industry and trade suffered no vital and permanent setback when the fall of the Empire in the West had removed the unified framework of civil and military defense, and left in its place a number of different, and often antagonistic, governmental units. Such proof, if it is to cover the economic life of western Europe, must be not only extensive, but representative, and typical of whole countries. The provinces of the later Roman Empire already exhibited marked variations, and the circumstances of the barbarian settlements greatly increased them. In Italy, the contrasting conditions of the Byzantine exarchate and the Lombard districts are

<hr>

[6] Historians mentioned in this paragraph: Max Weber (1864–1920) ranks as one of the most profound of German historians of his day; today we would call him a social scientist. Karl Bücher was a German economic historian. Beloch (1854–1929) and E. Meyer (1855–1930) were German authorities on the ancient world. [Editor's note]

well known, and for the latter the unsatisfactory nature of the sources has often been emphasised. . . . In France, regional differences are equally remarkable, and the unequal — and scanty — nature of the evidence forms an inadequate basis for the far-reaching conclusions of Pirenne's theory. The Germanic districts, for example, of the Merovingian realm rarely find mention in the sources, and the survival of Rhineland trade in the fifth and sixth centuries is incapable of proof. A principal part in that theory is played by the statements of Gregory of Tours, but the striking criticism of N. H. Baynes has gone far to invalidate the interpretation placed upon them, and his suggestion that the unity of the Mediterranean world was broken, not by the advance of Islam, but by the pirate fleet of Vandal Carthage, seems more in accordance with probability. Moreover, in face of the general picture of the barbarous conditions in France delineated by Gregory of Tours, stronger proofs than Pirenne has been able to adduce are required before we can be confident of the survival of a highly developed machinery of trade. It is not sufficient to point to examples of exotic imports as evidence of this. Easily portable luxuries — amber, jewels, beads — were carried enormous distances in prehistoric times, but such commerce belongs rather to the romance than to the everyday realities of economic life. Finally, the evidence for the continuance of the Roman educational system under the Merovings, to which Pirenne has devoted several studies, is not, in the opinion of the present writer, convincing.

Dopsch's theory has developed from his criticism of opposing views, and it may be suggested that this circumstance has led to a somewhat one-sided presentation of the facts, and not infrequently to over-statement. The quality of his voluminous evidence varies considerably, and much of it has already been called in question. In drawing attention to the immense variety of conditions which prevailed in western Europe during these centuries, and in modifying the generalisations which have been put forward concerning its social and economic life, Dopsch has performed an invaluable service. Whether these modifications are sufficiently far-reaching to establish a new and authoritative "pattern" of economic development is a more doubtful matter.

M. PIRENNE AND THE UNITY OF THE MEDITERRANEAN WORLD

NORMAN H. BAYNES

Norman H. Baynes (1877–   ), Britain's outstanding Byzantine scholar in our day, came to the field of history as he was approaching middle age. A barrister-at-law, during World War I he was confronted with a choice of continuing in the teaching and practice of law, or turning to the teaching and writing of history. For English historical scholarship his decision was a happy one; for close to thirty years he was a member of the teaching staff of University College, London, where he was held in great affection and high esteem. His scholarly work, extensive and arresting, which brought him many honors, including honorary degrees from Oxford and Cambridge, was largely devoted to Byzantine studies, or, as he preferred to call it, East Roman History. The selection which follows is from a book review, published in 1929, of the French edition of Pirenne's *Medieval Cities*.

FOR M. PIRENNE the unity of the Mediterranean world was maintained unbroken into the eighth century of our era: that unity was only shattered as a result of the Arab conquest of Africa. Upon the continent that theory has been vigorously canvassed and directly challenged; it gave rise, I understand, to the debate which most successfully enlivened the proceedings of the International Congress of Historical Studies at Oslo. To it British scholarship has paid little attention — a disquieting sign of that general lack of interest in the early European Middle Age which is now prevalent in this country. Yet the problem raised by M. Pirenne is of the greatest significance alike for the history of the later Roman Empire and for the understanding of the whole period of transition which separates the reign of Theodosius the Great from the age of Charlemagne. The central issue at stake is the position of Merovingian Gaul, and in particular the question of the part played by the Syrian merchants of the West in the economic life of the Merovingian kingdom. Here Gregory of Tours[1] is, of course, our principal authority. The *History of the Franks* is an extensive work and it will probably be admitted that it has its *longueurs*: the most blood-thirsty reader can become sated by the story of incessant assassinations. Thus it may be suspected that the *History* is more often consulted than it is read through from beginning to end. Yet it is only by such a reading that one can gain an impression of the range of Gregory's interests and contacts. After such a reading I should like to take this opportunity to record my own personal impressions. M. Pirenne writes "La Méditerranée ne perd

[1] Gregory of Tours, 539–594. His *History of the Franks* is regarded as one of the most important historical works of the early Middle Ages. [Editor's note]

From "M. Pirenne and the Unity of the Mediterranean World," in Norman H. Baynes, *Byzantine Studies and Other Essays* (University of London, The Athlone Press, London, 1955), pp. 310–316. Reprinted from *Journal of Roman Studies*, XIX (1929), by permission of the Society for the Promotion of Roman Studies.

pas son importance après la période des invasions. Elle reste pour les Germains ce qu'elle était avant leur arrivée: le centre même de l'Europe, le *mare nostrum*." ["The Mediterranean did not lose its importance after the period of the invasions. It remained for the Germans what it had been before their arrival: the very center of Europe, the *mare nostrum*."] In what sense and to what extent is this true? How far can we prove direct contact between, let us say, Antioch or Alexandria and the ports of Merovingian Gaul?

In the first place two remarks must be made: (i) Students of economics have been tempted to give to terms used in our medieval sources a modern significance which is foreign to their context. If a "merchant" is mentioned, they tend to presume that he is engaged in far-reaching, even transmarine, transactions. . . . [But] the merchant may be solely concerned with local trade. (ii) From the mention of "Syrians" in the Western sources during the early Middle Ages there is not infrequently drawn the inference that these eastern immigrants remained in close commercial relations with their country of origin, or that the population of these colonies was being constantly reinforced by new arrivals from the East . . . this presupposition underlies all M. Bréhier's work upon the subject.[2] That there was such commercial intercourse under the early Empire cannot be doubted: this it was which brought the Orientals to Western Europe. . . . Such intercourse continued through the fourth and into the early fifth century, but its persistence into the Middle Age of Merovingian Gaul cannot simply be assumed; the prior question must be asked: is there any justification for such an assumption?

Perhaps the best method of approach is to study Gregory's knowledge of foreign countries:[3] what is the range of his infor-

mation? Of affairs in Visigothic Spain he was fully informed: embassies were frequent, and he himself questioned Chilperic's envoys to Leuvigild on the condition of the Spanish Catholics. Agilan, Leuvigild's envoy, passed through Tours and disputed with Gregory, and the bishop was present at the banquet given by Oppila. Of N. Italy Gregory naturally knew something owing to the Frankish invasions of the country, but of S. Italy he seems to have known little: he can make the remarkable statement that Buccelin[4] captured Sicily and exacted tribute from it. Of Rome and of the Popes of the time we hear nothing, save of the appeal to John III in the case of the bishops Salonius and Sagittarius. [In the next book] however, we are given a long account of affairs in Rome, showing Gregory's readiness to be interested in the subject when information could be obtained. The reason for this sudden extension of the range of Gregory's vision lies in the fact that a deacon of Tours, who had been sent on a mission to Rome to acquire relics of the saints, had just returned from Italy. If the reader will consider the character of the information there recorded, and Gregory's general silence on Roman matters he will, I think, infer that Gaul was at this time not in regular contact with Italy. I myself cannot believe that ships and traders were customarily passing between Italy and Merovingian Gaul.[5]

If we pass to the history of the Roman Empire in the Eastern Mediterranean the result is curiously similar. Of Justinian we

---

[4] Buccelin was a German chieftain; he and his men were crushed by Narses (one of Justinian's generals), near Capua in 554. [Editor's note]

[5] Individuals mentioned in this and subsequent paragraphs: Leuvigild was king of the Visigoths, 568–586. Chilperic and Sigebert were sons of the Merovingian king of the Franks, Chlotar I; they and their two brothers waged civil war over the division of the kingdom following their father's death in 561. Tiberius II (578–582) and Maurice (582–602) were Eastern Roman Emperors. Childebert II, son of Sigebert and of the famous Brunhild (Visigoth princess) was king of the Franks, 575–596. Gundovald, illegitimate son of Chlotar I, revolted against Childebert II and was crushed by Brunhild. [Editor's note]

[2] Louis Bréhier is a French authority on Byzantine history. His best known work is *Le Monde Byzantin*, 3 vols. (Paris, 1947–1950). [Editor's note]

[3] The references to *The History of the Franks*, supplied by Baynes, are omitted. [Editor's note]

hear nothing save the appointment of Narses in place of Belisarius in Italy and the campaign in Spain. But of Justin's reign we learn more: of his character, of the capture by the Persians of Syrian Antioch — Antioch is placed in Egypt! — of the Persian War and of the association by Justin of Tiberius as colleague. This sudden expansion of the narrative is due to the fact that envoys of Sigebert returned at this time to Gaul from an embassy to the imperial court at Constantinople. From the reign of Tiberius we are given legends of the emperor's liberality, an account of the plot to dethrone him in favour of Justinian, Justin's nephew, and of his Persian War; but of the stubborn defence of Sirmium against the Avars Gregory knows nothing. The source of his information and the reason for his silence may be conjectured from the fact that Chilperic's embassy to Tiberius returned to Gaul, it would appear, in the year 580. The operations against the Avars belong to the years 580–582. We take up the eastern story once more with the death of Tiberius and the accession of Maurice. Here again the information doubtless came through the imperial envoys who brought a subsidy of 50,000 pieces of gold to induce Childebert to attack the Lombards in Italy. Gregory's interest in the affairs of the East when he could obtain first-hand knowledge of happenings there is shown from his account of the capture of Antioch by the Persians derived from the refugee bishop Simon, the Armenian. The conclusion which would seem to result from this analysis is that Gregory had no regular source of information for eastern affairs such as would have been furnished by traders had they been in continued relation with the ports of the eastern empire.

Further, it is remarkable that Childebert's envoy to Constantinople, Grippo, did not sail directly to the East, but went to Carthage and there awaited the praefect's pleasure before he was allowed to proceed to the imperial court. M. Bréhier points out that Gundovald left Constantinople and ultimately arrived at Marseilles. True, but Gregory gives no hint of his route; did he, too, travel by way of Carthage?

How far does Gregory's own narrative support this negative inference? There is a Syrian merchant at Bordeaux who possessed a relic of St. Sergius, but at a time when pilgrimages and relic hunting were familiar who shall say how this finger of the saint reached Bordeaux? There were Syrians and Jews in Paris, and one of them, a merchant, by name Eusebius, secured by bribes the bishopric; a Syrian of Tours helped Gregory to translate into Latin the legend of the Seven Sleepers of Ephesus, but there is nothing to connect them with their Syrian homeland. In Merovingian Gaul the Bretons had ships; we hear of a ship owned by a Jew coasting from Nice to Marseilles; the Visigoths of Spain possessed ships, a ship sailing from Spain "with the usual merchandise" arrives at Marseilles, while ships sailing from Gaul to Galicia are plundered by Leuvigild. Nowhere, so far as I can see, in the work of Gregory of Tours is there any suggestion of a *direct* contact of Merovingian Gaul with the eastern Mediterranean. If Justinian was constrained to resort to measures of fiscal oppression to compel shipowners to trade with the new imperial conquests in Italy and Africa, it is hardly likely that East Roman merchants would readily sail to the ports of Gaul. That products from the East reached Merovingian Gaul is clear, but the problem is whence did they come *directly*? Was it from imperial territory in Spain or from Carthage.

My own belief is that the unity of the Mediterranean world was broken by the pirate fleet of Vandal Carthage and that the shattered unity was never restored. A Merovingian might have pepper to his meat, the wine of Gaza might be a bait to lure a man to his assassination but Gaul of the Merovingians, so far as vital contacts with the empire were concerned, was from the first marooned. Gregory with all his advantages only gained occasional fragments of information upon the doings of Romania. . . .

If, then, the view which I have endeavoured to set forth has any foundation, it is misleading to state that for the Franks of the sixth century the Mediterranean still remained "mare nostrum"; we can only accept with qualifications the statement that "the great Mediterranean commerce which flourished in Gaul during the Late Empire subsisted into the 6th and even into the 7th century"; it is only true at a remove that "of Byzantium, of Asia Minor and of Egypt Jewish merchants, but more especially Syrian merchants continued to supply it (Gaul) with luxury goods, with precious fabrics, with fine wines."[6]

[6] The quotations are from F. Vercauteren (another Belgian historian) and from Pirenne. Baynes quotes them in French. [Editor's note]

MOHAMMED AND CHARLEMAGNE:
A Revision

ROBERT S. LOPEZ

Robert S. Lopez, born and educated in Italy, came to the United States shortly before World War II; during that conflict he served with the Italian Section of the Office of War Information. He has since become recognized as one of the most active and competent of the younger medievalists in this country. He has taught at Brooklyn College and at Columbia and is presently at Yale. One of his many research interests has been in the field of medieval trade in the Mediterranean and he has accordingly been much involved in the Pirenne controversy. One of his early contributions, an important one, appeared in *Speculum* in 1943 and this article is here reproduced in its entirety, save for the omission of a few foreign terms. Professor Lopez now considers this paper only "a pioneer effort in a direction which was explored more thoroughly since its publication." It is nonetheless valuable in illustrating the character of the controversy fifteen years ago. It is also a clear expression of many of the fundamental issues in the problem, and if certain of the answers he then gave have been since superseded it is in part from further research by Professor Lopez himself. Some of this he sets forth in the second extract which is taken from a paper which he read at the Tenth International Congress of Historical Sciences convening in Rome in 1955.

IT IS not my purpose to challenge the core of Pirenne's conclusions. *Mahomet et Charlemagne,* and Dopsch's *Grundlagen* — however much one may disagree on point of details and on range of implications — have helped historians to realize that their traditional division of ages was wrong: Germanic invasions did not mark the beginning of a new era; Arab invasions did.

This is undoubtedly true in so far as history of culture is concerned. The great push of the Germans had been preceded by long interpenetration, and was followed by thorough fusion of the newcomers into the mass of the conquered people. The followers of Alaric, Theodoric and Clovis neither wanted to nor could break the moral unity of the Western Empire, and its connections with the East. They only gave a political expression to those particularisms which were already cracking the surface of the old Roman edifice without breaking its deep foundations. The Latin language and Latin literature, however much their already advanced barbarization may have been precipitated by the impact of rude invaders, remained as the common background of European culture. The greatest achievements of the mediaeval "Germanized" world, the Church and the Empire, were either a heritage or an imitation of Roman institutions. As soon as

From "Mohammed and Charlemagne: A Revision," *Speculum,* XVIII (January, 1943), 14–38. By permission of the Medieval Academy of America, Cambridge, Mass.

Europe was again able to produce something great and original, Roman peoples again took the lead. *Niebelungennot* and the wooden buildings of the Germans were forgotten for Romanesque and French ("Gothic") architecture, and for the Italian *Divina Commedia*.

On the other hand, wherever the Arabs stepped on Romanic soil (except in Spain and in Sicily, outposts which they held for too short a time), they eradicated the classic roots forever. A slow but sweeping revolution won over the masses in Syria, Egypt, and North Africa to a new civilization, whose language and religion (these typical expressions of a people's soul) were the language and the religion of the conquerors. There was no Arab Romanesque architecture, and no Arab Imperium. Even where there was imitation, an original blend was formed out of three cultures — Graeco-Roman, Persian, and Semitic.

However, neither Pirenne nor Dopsch lays as much stress on cultural relations as they do on economic and social conditions. I shall not discuss here the views of Dopsch. Let us remark only that, while his thesis cannot be slighted as an element in the understanding of the early Middle Ages, his documentation has been recognized as too scanty and questionable for the wide inferences which many followers of Dopsch have drawn. Are the foundations of Pirenne's economic theory more solid? At first, one cannot but be struck by the four "disappearances" which he pointed out as the symptoms of a disruption of the economic unity of the Mediterranean countries after the Arabic invasions. Papyrus, Oriental luxury cloths, spices, and gold currency shrank gradually to the Eastern part of the Mediterranean; under the Carolingians, Europe had almost entirely abandoned their use. Pirenne's documentation is striking.

And yet, on a close examination, it appears that the four "disappearances" were not contemporary either with the Arab advance or with each other; indeed, it is not exact to speak of disappearances. Papyrus

was manufactured exclusively in Egypt, and this province was conquered by the Arabs between 639 and 641. But it was only in 692 that the Merovingian chancery ceased to use papyrus for its official documents. Other powers of the Christian world (as we shall see better later) continued to use papyrus for several centuries afterwards. Gold money ceased to be struck in France, apparently, only in the second half of the eighth century; in Italy, it came to an abrupt end in or about 800 — a date of no importance for the Caliphate, but a great date for Europe. Furthermore, there was a brilliant resumption of gold currency under Louis the Pious; and gold kept an important place among the means of exchange, at least in Italy and in England, under the form of foreign and imitated coins, metallic dust, and ingots. A Belgian scholar, Sabbe, has recently proved that there was still a current of importation of Oriental cloth during the ninth and tenth centuries. Although his essay does not cover specifically the trade in spices, occasional references to it lead us to draw a similar conclusion.

In the presence of these circumstances, it seems difficult to maintain a "catastrophic" thesis, and to envisage Arab conquests as the cause of a sudden collapse in international trade — which, in turn, would have produced sweeping social and economic internal revolutions. In other words, there were no sudden changes as an immediate and direct repercussion of the Arab conquests. International trade was not swept away at one stroke, and "closed economy" did not spring up at once in the regions outside the gleam of the Moslem Crescent. However, new trends slowly asserted themselves in the economy of the Western world. These trends should be related to conditions existing in the Arab or Byzantine world, for any disturbance in the European supply of Oriental wares is likely to originate in events occurring somewhere in the East.

We shall have a first clue if we take into account a circumstance which Pirenne and

his followers seem to have overlooked:
Three of the "disappearing" goods — gold
currency, luxury fabrics, and papyrus —
were state monopolies, and their sale had
been subjected to special restrictions ever
since the Roman Empire. A short survey
of these restrictions will be necessary to
understand the whole problem.

Currency has been, and still is, a public
monopoly in almost all civilized states. This
depends chiefly on two causes. On the one
hand, it is felt that issuing the most tangi-
ble and popular symbol of wealth should be
a prerogative of the sovereign power. On
the other hand, it is deemed that state control is the best means to give to the paramount instrument of exchanges universal
credit, a stable standard, and a surety
against counterfeiting. Thus currency is at
the same time a sovereign function — what
the Middle Ages called a "regale" — and a
device of public interest.

Besides, money can become a source of
public income (in other words, a fiscal monopoly) if the state can make the people
accept coins at a higher price than the
actual content of their bullion plus cost of
coinage. But this development of currency,
no matter how often a state can resort to it,
is a pathologic phenomenon which sooner
or later defeats the very aims of currency,
and makes it unfit as a means of exchange.
In the Roman Republic and Empire,
money had always been both a symbol of
sovereign power and a device for public
interest. Debasements had taken place repeatedly, but the notion that coinage might
be a mere source of income for the state,
variable at the will of the rulers, was never
accepted.

However, there was a distinction and a
hierarchy of metals, the origins of which
can be traced back to similar regulations of
the Persian and Seleucid monarchies. The
state mints for copper and silver were sometimes leased out, at least until a law (393
A.D.) prohibited such a practice and revoked all the earlier grants; but gold mints
were never leased out. Silver and copper
money, with both standard and types differ-

ent from those of the state currency, were
allowed to some autonomous municipalities
for local use; but gold was never struck in
local mints. The Senate of the Republic
struck every sort of money; but after the
rise of Augustus, it was left with the right
to strike copper only. Gold and silver state
coinage became a monopoly of the Emperor, who also had coppers struck occasionally in the provinces.

When the "Principate" was transformed
into a "Dominate," both Senate coppers and
autonomous municipal coinage of silver
and copper were driven out in a few years
by the extraordinary emissions of debased
coins in the imperial mints. No definite
order of dissolution seems to have been en-
acted; but the mint of the Senate was never
reopened (except under the Ostrogoths),
and local coinage had only sporadic and
short-lived reappearances, as long as the
Roman and the Byzantine Empires lasted.
This extension of imperial monopoly to
every kind of money and every metal must
be connected with the progress of absolutism. Forging coins, striking them in private
workshops, refusing old and worn imperial
money was regarded as a "sacrilegium," or
an act of "laesa maiestas," because it im-
plied an outrage to the effigy of the sovereign impressed on the coins. But motives
of public interest were almost as influential
as this new stress on the sacred character
of money-regale, for in the fourth, fifth, and
sixth centuries there was such an increase
in forgeries, that the only remedy seemed
to be a thorough and undiscriminating state
monopolization.

The rise of barbaric autonomous states
formally subjected to imperial suzerainty
again raised the problem of local currency.
Once more, the view of the Emperors (as
stated by Procopius and confirmed by the
extant coins) was that barbarian kings
should be entitled to strike both copper and
silver with their own effigies and names;
but gold could be lawfully struck only with
the portrait and name of the *Roman* Emperor. Along with this pretension went the
Byzantine claim that no foreign prince

could call himself Emperor (Basileus) on equal terms with the autocrat of Constantinople.

Altogether, these pretensions suffered no serious challenge for a long time. The Vandals and the Ostrogoths never struck gold coins with the effigies of their sovereigns. The Visigoths and the Lombards began to issue gold with their king's portrait only very late, when they had no longer anything to fear from the Emperor's wrath. Theodebert I, the Merovingian, while at war against Justinian the Great, struck some personal gold coins which roused the indignation of Procopius; it is true that Justinian, on his side, hurt the feelings of the Frankish ruler by assuming the title of "Francicus," which amounted to a claim to a triumph over him. After Theodebert, no Merovingian king struck gold with his own portrait for some years. When this "usurpation" was committed again, the Emperor needed Frankish alliance against the Lombards, too badly to raise complaints. A similar calculation must have led the Basileis not only to overlook the gold coinage of the Ethiopian kings of Aksum, but to bestow on them the title of Basileis in the official correspondence. The common rival of Byzantium and Aksum, the Sasanian "Shahan Sha" (King of the Kings), was also called Basileus and regarded as an equal by the Basileus of Constantinople. But he eventually abandoned gold currency, to the great satisfaction of the Byzantine court. His pride could find a compensation in the yearly tribute that the Empire had to pay to him.

The success of Constantinople in matters of money-regale was not entirely due to the prestige and the power of the Emperors. In Western Europe not only gold, but even the less valuable metals continued to be struck in large amounts with the portrait of the Emperor, because the populace, accustomed to the traditional types, was reluctant to accept coins of an unusual appearance. In Persia and in some of the barbaric states, gold was of little use anyway, because the exchanges were generally of a modest amount, and silver was more suitable for the common needs. Finally, the title of "rex" had an equivalent in all the Indo-European languages, while that of "imperator" was proper to Latin only.

Nonetheless, it is an undoubted fact that the early Germanic rulers recognized some moral hierarchic superiority of the Emperors in several other respects. As for gold currency, we cannot say that German kings did not care about it because they had no "regalian" notion. On the contrary, the barbaric states of Western Europe as a rule maintained a state monopoly of money. Even more, both Visigoths and Lombards apparently followed closely the developments of eastern Roman law on that matter. As soon as the Byzantine Empire changed the penalty to be enforced on money-counterfeiters, the same modification was introduced by Receswinth in Spain and by Rothari in Italy.[1] Besides, Rothari seems to have re-organized the Lombard mints according to an administrative reform of emperor Heraclius. Only the Merovingian state followed an opposite course: the very notion of state monopoly was slowly forgotten, and private moneyers began to strike on private order coins bearing no other marks than the moneyer's signature, the customer's name, and the place of emission. This was because the Merovingian monarchies during the seventh century underwent a steady decline of internal cohesion and international relations.

The inclusion of some kinds of cloths and jewelry in the "regalian" monopolies will not seem surprising, if we remember that in the late Roman and Byzantine Empires the sovereign impersonated the state, and made himself a superhuman being to the eyes of the populace, even by his exterior appearance. Thus imperial garments and jewelry were symbols of the nation, almost like our flag. An offense against them was really a threat to the stability of

---

[1] Receswinth (d. 672) was king of the Visigoths; Rothari (d. 652) was king of the Lombards, particularly important for his codification of Lombard customary law. [Editor's note]

the regime, and the protection extended to them could be regarded as a matter of public interest. This notion had already appeared in the Oriental monarchies, where the worship of the sovereign was taken as a matter of course. But the Romans were proud of their personal freedom and dignity. As long as they were allowed, they spoke of "our plebeian purple" (as opposed to the other peoples' "royal purple") with a satisfaction similar to our pride in free speech and popular government.

Only the Late Empire introduced the worship of the living autocrat, and destroyed even the exterior forms of liberty. Purple-dyed and gold-embroidered cloths, and jewelry of several categories were brought under "regalian" restrictions. A hierarchy of materials, parallel to the hierarchy of offices, was established in this monopoly, as it had been established in currency. A certain kind of purple and some special jewels were allowed only to God, to the saints, and to the sovereigns. Other ceremonial garments were reserved to high officers; by that means, they shared in the veneration owed to the Emperor. Other cloths — even some dyed with purple or embroidered with gold and silk— continued to be permitted to the commoners. This arrangement was subject to fluctuations, for, in the fifth century, there were innumerable crimes of "majesty"— that is, private use of imperial garments and jewels. The only remedy appeared to be to extend the state monopoly to a much larger field than the strictly "tabooed" objects. Little by little, as the citizens made up their minds to reserve some ornaments to the sacred person of the sovereign and to his dignitaries, unnecessary restrictions were lifted.

When the Western Empire was dismembered, the Byzantine Emperors were able to defend their monopoly of ceremonial garments better than that of gold currency. As a matter of fact, some of the raw materials (silk, several qualities of purple-dyes, pearls and other precious stones) could not be found in Western Europe. Furthermore,

the goldsmiths and clothiers of the Barbarians were often very skilled in their own way, but they could not reproduce the patterns of Roman aulic art. Thus the Empire had practically a monopoly of production and supply. Control of exportation was sufficient to prevent Barbarian leaders from robing themselves in garments which they were not supposed to wear. Not only "regalian" considerations, but a "premercantilistic" outlook led the Emperors to enforce on exporters even more drastic restrictions than those enforced at home. It was not convenient to allow gold, precious stones, and secrets of textile industries to be taken out of the state.

On the other hand, the Emperors themselves used to buy off Barbarian rulers by gifts of ceremonial garments and jewels. Such gifts were cautiously dealt out, lest their value depreciated. Besides, no imperial mantles and crowns were given, but only ornaments allowed to Byzantine high officers. Thus the donors could feel that they were enlisting Barbarians in the army of Byzantine officers and vassals, while the grantees usually felt pleased and exalted with the gifts. Likewise, the gift of regalian ornaments to churches and clergy in the West was one of the weapons of the Byzantine ecclesiastic diplomacy. But the amount of objects obtained by that means, captured as war prizes, or smuggled into Western Europe with the help of bribed imperial manufacturers and customs-officers, could never be very large. Furthermore, some of the Barbaric peoples (although *not* all of them) cared little for the shining, but somewhat effeminate apparel of the Basileis. They took more pride in their national fur garments, spurned by the Romans, and in Germanic parade armors.

The situation was different in Persia and in Ethiopia, where both raw materials and finished objects could be secured without Byzantine intermediaries. In these countries, the local ceremonial costumes were similar to those of the Eastern Empire; indeed, the latter repeatedly borrowed Persian aulic fashions. Apparently the Basileis were wise enough not to put forward any monop-olistic claims as regards Ethiopia and Persia. At any rate, it was less wounding to see the sovereigns of those very ancient states dressed in purple than the unpedigreed rulers of provinces recently belonging to the Romans.

Papyrus had also been subject to restric-tions under the Ptolemies, but on a differ-ent ground. In Hellenistic Egypt nearly all the wares of some value were under fiscal monopoly, no matter whether the stability of the regime or the public welfare required it or not. While some of these goods were directly produced and sold by state agents, more often private entrepreneurs leased out portions of the monopolistic rights in one or more provinces. There was no absolute monopoly on papyrus production, although many fields were directly cultivated and exploited by the crown. But the private producers, apparently, could sell only to the king the best qualities of papyrus ("basilikē chartē," royal papyrus). Moreover, public notaries were expected to write their instru-ments on this kind of papyrus, and to pay a tax on every deed.

It seems that these provisions did not aim at protecting against forgeries of docu-ments; they were only one of the number-less restrictions by which the Ptolemies fleeced their flock. This is why the Romans, systematically opposed to fiscal monopolies, seem to have removed the obstacles against free commerce. But they maintained the duty on notarial instruments as a sort of certification fee.

This tax, however, contained the germ of the elements for the later growth of a state monopoly with a purpose of public interest. As a matter of fact, during the fifth and sixth centuries the increasing for-geries of documents led the Emperors to issue a set of provisions which revived and completed the ancient restrictions. Notaries public were obliged again to use only "basilikē chartē" for their deeds. This time, the restrictions did not aim primarily at securing an outlet for the state production of papyrus, but rather at bringing under state control the drawing of legal docu-ments. The right of selling state papyrus apparently had been leased out to private citizens in the provinces; now such leases were revoked. Justinian ordered that no notarial instrument drawn in Constanti-nople should be recognized as authentic, unless each roll of papyrus had an un-touched first sheet, which contained the subscription of the state officers attached to papyrus administration. Another guarantee of authenticity was the heading, to be com-piled according to a definite formula, with the names of both the ruling sovereign and the consuls. Particular cautions were adopted for state documents: Purple ink must be used for the signature of the Em-peror; golden seals, with an effigy of the sovereign like that on golden coins, were also attached to the most important im-perial documents. Again, for state docu-ments issued by members of the imperial family or by subordinate officers a special, but inferior set of precautions was adopted. Silver ink, silver, leaden or clay seals, and other exterior features pointed out the im-portance of the various writs, in proportion to the authority of the writer.

By that way a new field of monopolies was opened. Obviously their aim could be qualified as one of public interest. The fact that the Emperor, and his officers, lent in different ways the prestige of their names and portraits, caused restrictions and cau-tions concerning state and notarial instru-ments to take on the character of regales. Forging imperial documents signed with purple ink, or even using such an ink for private writing, was regarded as a crime of majesty, committed "tyrannico spiritu," and liable to capital penalty. Forgeries of less solemn charters were punished by maiming of a hand.

These laws apparently were taken over, in a simplified form, both by the Visigoths and the Lombards, at the same time as Heraclius' legislation on currency. The Pope and the bishops, who followed Ro-man law, seem to have uniformed their correspondence to the rules set in Constantinople. Since the production of papyrus was strictly localized in the Byzantine province of Egypt, whoever used papyrus (even outside the borders of the Empire) had to bow to the imperial monopoly. On the other hand, as the monopoly was one of production, and not of use like the clothing monopoly, the supply of lawful writing material to the Western chanceries and notaries went on unhampered.

The appearance of the Arabs among the great powers of the Mediterranean did not, at first, bring about such a revolution in the system of regalian monopolies as it could have. To be sure, the conquerors could seize in Egypt and in Syria two Byzantine state mints, a number of dye-houses for ceremonial garments, and the whole output of papyrus. But work was carried on almost as usual, with unchanged staff and unaltered standard of production. The Arabs, as a rule, conserved the existing state of things wherever they had no definite reasons to change it. They were slow in setting up regalian monopolies, for they had none at home. When they did, however, they were not awkward and half-hearted imitators, like the Germans. On the contrary, the Arabs built a solid state organization out of an original blend of Byzantine, Persian and national institutions.

According to an early tradition, the Prophet praised himself for having "left to Mesopotamia its dirhem and its hafīz, to Syria its mudd and its dīnār, to Egypt its ardeb and its dīnār." As a matter of fact, the bulk of circulation in the early Arab Caliphate was formed by pre-Arabic Sasanian, Byzantine and a few Himyarite (South-Arabic) coins, plus new money of the Empire which was currently imported by merchants. This currency of foreign origin was soon augmented with domestic imitations, privately struck, of Persian and Byzantine coins.

We have already remarked that the same phenomenon occurred with the Germans. But in the Arab Empire, where civilization was older and money exchanges were larger, the period before autonomous cur-

rency would not have lasted so long, but for peculiar delaying reasons. All the moneys in use at the time of the Arab conquest bore some representations of living objects, and such figures were unwelcome (although not altogether prohibited) because of the Islamic religious principles. On the other hand, it would have been almost impossible to get the subject peoples to accept suddenly money with simple inscriptions. 'Ali,[2] the champion of the old indigenous orthodoxy, tried to put out some non-figured coins but his attempt died with him.

The simplest solution by far was tolerating the maintenance of the traditional, unofficial currency. Thus the blame for the figures could fall upon the foreign rulers and the unauthorized private moneyers who had struck the coins. At the most, some emblems of the Gentile religion were completed (or replaced after erasure) with legends praising Allah and Mohammed. Moreover, even this practice was not altogether immune from the censure of the most rigid lawyers, because such coins with their sacred formula were exposed to falling into the hands of men legally impure. At last, under Caliph Mu'āwiyah,[3] a few coppers were issued on which the portrait of the Basileus holding a cross was replaced by that of the Caliph brandishing a sword. But gold currency, the pride of the Empire, was not affected; and Mu'āwiyah gave a greater satisfaction to the Emperor, by binding himself to the payment of a yearly tribute.

While the currency, destined mainly to be handled by the Gentile subjects, was not modified for a long time, the Arabs soon conformed the drawing of their own state documents to the precepts of Islam. Seals had been largely used, even for private correspondence, before Mohammed; there-

[2] 'Ali was a son-in-law of Mohammed and was caliph, 655–661. [Editor's note]

[3] Mu'āwiyah was the first Omayyad caliph (661–680) and one of the great Moslem statesmen. He developed a centralized autocratic administration, with headquarters at Damascus, which unified the Moslem world. [Editor's note]

fore we may cast some doubt on a tradition, according to which the Prophet had a seal engraved only when he was told that the Emperor would not read his letters if unsealed. At any rate, we have full evidence that the seal of the Caliphate was protected by a special "regalian" notion, as early as the time of 'Umar I,[4] the conqueror of Syria and Egypt. A little later, Mu'āwiyah organized an Office of the State Seal, on the model of a similar Sasanian institution. The Byzantine papyrus manufacturers in Egypt were maintained under state control, although it is not clear whether or not the imperial regulation for monopoly of the best qualities of papyrus was enforced by the Arabs without modifications.

For internal use the Arabs adapted the preparation of chancery materials and records to the needs of their own state and religious organization. It is true that some figures of animals (and, occasionally, even of men), as well as the cross, were left on the seals and the protocols, as merely decorative adornments. But the name of the Basileus and the Christian formulae were soon replaced by the name of the Caliph and Islamic sentences. However, on the papyri which were exported to the Empire the Christian workers of the papyrus factories replaced the name of the Basileus, which obviously could not be written on the protocol (in Arabic "tirāz"), by an invocation to the Trinity. This arrangement, worked out or tolerated by the Islamic officers, was advantageous for both the Empire and the Caliphate. The former secured the usual supply of a material necessary to the chancery and the notaries — for Justinian's laws, which ordered the use of papyrus with untouched protocols, were still in force. The Arabs, on their side, drew large profits from this exportation, and, in that way, secured a continuous inflow of that Byzantine gold which formed the bulk of their currency.

An arrangement of the same kind was worked out for embroidered ceremonial cloths. It was an Arabic use — modeled, apparently, on a Persian custom, for no evidence of a similar practice can be found on Byzantine cloths before the so-called Byzantine Middle Ages — that a "tirāz" with the name of the Caliph and religious sentences should be embroidered on all ceremonial cloths. But on the tissues which were exported into Christian countries only an invocation to the Trinity was applied.

This unwritten compromise was broken by the real founder of the Arab administrative machinery, 'Abd al-Malik.[5] He could not think of reforms in the first years of his reign, for he was engaged in an all-out civil war against 'Abdallāh ibn-az-Zubair; indeed, for the sake of peace he had even to increase the yearly tribute to the Emperor (686 or 687 A.D.). But, as soon as the danger was overcome, the Caliph resolutely inaugurated a new policy, with the double aim of consolidating the central power, and of offering some satisfaction to the orthodox Arab element, from which came the main support of the enemies of his dynasty. The brother of ibn-az-Zubair had coined a number of small silver dirhems; 'Abd al-Malik ordered them to be broken up, thus showing a decidedly "regalian" viewpoint. Then he ordered the invocation to the Trinity and the cross on the "tirāz" of the papyri and cloths destined for export replaced by Moslem formulae. Emperor Justinian II, who evidently did not want to break the advantageous treaty of 686–687, tried repeatedly to obtain the withdrawal of those provisions by large gifts; he always met with a refusal. Finally his rash and violent character prevailed over diplomatic tact. He threatened the Caliph with putting an outrageous inscription against the Prophet on his gold coins, which (as he thought) the Arabs could not help using.

But the Caliph was now the stronger. As a reprisal, he entirely prohibited the exportation of papyrus, and inaugurated a

---

[4] 'Umar I was the caliph (634–644) under whom Islam expanded religiously and politically over Syria, Egypt, and Persia. [Editor's note]

[5] 'Abd al-Malik was caliph 685–705. [Editor's note]

national gold and silver currency, of the same type as the figured coppers of Mu'āwiyah. He thought of making the new coins acceptable to the Byzantine pride (or was it a refinement of jest?) by sending the first specimen of this new money as a part of the yearly tribute; besides, he promised to keep accepting the Byzantine gold currency in his own states. But when Justinian saw his own humiliation brought home to him, under the form of the coins bearing the name and the portrait of 'Abd al-Malik, he decided that the only issue left was war. Unfortunately, he was abandoned on the battlefield by the contingent of Slavs, on whom he relied. The Arabs, who had hoisted on their lances the broken treaty, gained a complete victory.

Nevertheless, the pretensions of the Byzantine rulers were satisfied in a way. The portrait of a Caliph on coins hurt the feelings of the orthodox "fukaha" as much as those of the Basileus, although the reasons for complaint were different. 'Abd al-Malik had succeeded in introducing into circulation a national type of coin; he soon took a further step, and had money coined like that of 'Ali, without any figure or personal symbol. After a short period of transition, when both figured and non-figured coins circulated together, the new type, bearing only pious inscriptions, affirmed itself. Ever since, the currency of Moslem dynasties has been without figures, with only a few exceptions. Even the recollection that there had been Islamic figured coins was eventually lost.

It would be incautious to dismiss the whole history of this "regalian" war by ascribing it to the "foolishness" of Justinian and to the "diabolic shrewdness" of 'Abd al-Malik, as do some later Byzantine chroniclers, bitterly adverse to the Emperor. To be sure, Justinian II was one of the worst men who ever sat on the Byzantine throne. But the war was more than a collision between a hot and cool head. It was a challenge between an old civilization, proud of its religious tradition and world power, and a new state, which had to make room

for the set-up of its own sacred formulae and sovereign prerogatives. A few years later, when the successor of Justinian, Philippicus, inaugurated a religious policy sharply hostile to the Pope, the Romans showed their solidarity with the latter by rejecting all the documents and the coins bearing the seal or the portrait of the impious Basileus. This proves that now the respect for the regalian character of moneys was not merely an artificial imposition of the rulers, but — let us repeat it — a popular feeling comparable with our reverence for the national flag.

The regalian notion of currency and of "tirāz" (both on ceremonial cloths and on public documents) almost at once took deep roots in the Caliphate, and in the various Moslem states which sprang up on its farthest provinces. Monopolistic state factories were established everywhere, with the same functions as those of the Byzantine Empire. The sovereign, and some members of his family or of his court appointed by him, reserved to themselves the right to put their names on the inscriptions of regalian objects. A hierarchy of materials in each kind of monopolies, corresponding to the hierarchy of officers, was established by custom if not, perhaps, by law: Gold — silver — copper for coins; different qualities of garments; probably, also different kinds of charters. To be sure, restrictions were never as extended as in the Empire. To give only some instances, mints were often leased out; in Egypt, state textile manufactures were set up only to give the finishing touch to cloths prepared in private workshops; the maiming penalty for infringers of regalian monopolies was suggested and enforced on several occasions, but it could never prevail against the stubborn hostility of nationalistic lawyers. But, altogether, the new regalian policy of Moslem rulers after 'Abd al-Malik stressed the same points which so far had been maintained by the Greeks.

As regards papyrus, the Arabs were in the same position as the Byzantine Empire before the loss of Egypt. They had the monopoly of production; if the other countries wanted any papyrus at all, they had to accept it as it was produced by the Moslem factories. Rather than waive the old laws on chancery and notarial instruments, the Basileis seem to have adapted themselves to the new situation. They continued to use papyrus, as is demonstrated by the earliest letter of a Byzantine Emperor of which an original fragment has come down to us (beginning of the ninth century). But, since the manufacturers no longer inscribed on the protocols the invocation to the Trinity, the Emperors transferred this invocation to the heading of the documents. Only in the tenth century, when Egypt itself ceased to manufacture papyrus because paper had replaced it all over the Arab states, was it necessary for the Greek chancery to adopt parchment.

The Roman regulation for the drawing of authentic documents was generally observed by the Popes, the Church, and the Byzantine territories of Italy. For instance, the consular date is found on most of the Papal documents, and on many private sources of the Roman region, until the first years of the tenth century. Papyrus was the only material used for formal Papal charters until the end of that century — with only one exception — and did not disappear entirely until 1057. A bull of John VII (year 876), which has been preserved with parts of the original protocol, bears on it the invocation to Allah, according to the regulation of 'Abd al-Malik. Papyrus was also widely used by bishops until the late eighth century; indeed, we know at least one episcopal letter written on that material as late as 977. We know many Roman private documents on papyrus of the same period; the last one is of 998. Urban documents of Ravenna, a Byzantine city until 751, and, later a center of studies in Roman Law, are on papyrus until the middle of the tenth century. Those are the instances which we can ascertain; on the other hand, the very largest part of papyri from Western Europe has certainly not come down to us, because this writing material, unlike parchment, is extremely perishable except in a dry climate. In conclusion, we can well say that *wherever the Roman regulation was observed, the disappearance of papyrus was not caused by the Arab conquests, but by the victory of paper three centuries later*.

In the barbaric states, however, Roman law was melting away. No consular dates are found in the secular documents of Lombard, Italy, France, and Germany. In a few private charters the words "sub die consule," without any indication of the consul's name, are the only relics of a forgotten formula, added by sheer force of habit. Force of habit led the Merovingian royal chancery to use imported papyrus *until 692*, although parchment, which could be easily produced at home, began occasionally to be used from 670 on. But *in 692* the embargo enforced by 'Abd al-Malik cut the supply entirely for some time. When this embargo was lifted, the Merovingian chancery did not go back to a costly material which had been purchased only out of respect to a vanishing tradition.

Unfortunately, no original documents of the Lombard chancery have come down to us. But all our knowledge of them, although indirect, leads us to think that not only the royal charters, but even those of the dukes were written on papyrus. This may explain why they all have perished. On the other hand, the earliest Italian private document on parchment which has come down to us, a notarial deed from Piacenza, dates from 716 — that is, twenty-eight years later than the Arab embargo. We may infer that the tradition of Roman law was still the stronger in Italy, in so far as state and church documents were concerned. But the reform of 'Abd al-Malik probably affected private instruments in Italy in the same way as it affected royal charters in France. In Germany, too, the earliest documents on parchment which have been preserved are of the second quarter of the eighth century. Thus it would seem that *where Roman legal traditions declined, the introduction of parchment for royal or notarial documents was not brought about*

directly by the Arab conquest of Egypt,
but by the organization of Arab state
monopolies, fifty years later.

When we compare Merovingian and
Carolingian currency, we are naturally led
to regard those two periods as separated by
a sharp contrast. First we have mainly
golden coins with a portrait; then we find
chiefly silver coins with an inscription.
However, the transition took place over a
long time. The output of silver coins became
abundant in France as early as the last years
of the sixth century — long before Mohammed and the decline of the Merovingians.
On the other hand, it is true that the
proportion of gold in circulation decreased
steadily under the late Merovingians, and
that no gold at all seems to have been struck
by Pepin the Short (though we cannot
exclude that some such coin may be eventually yielded by a new find); but gold
money was struck under Charlemagne and,
even more, under Louis the Pious. Likewise, the shift from figured to non-figured
money was gradual and progressive during
the sixth and seventh centuries. We have
no figured coins of Pepin, but we have
many of Charlemagne and Louis the Pious.

A connection of this gradual, though
interrupted decrease of gold coins with a
steady decrease in the volume of exchanges
cannot be doubted. On the other hand, the
decline of portraiture on coins must be
connected with both the general decline of
art, and the decadence of the sovereign
power. Silver is more convenient than gold
for small exchanges; unskilled moneyers
will prefer easy epigraphic types, unless a
sovereign insists on advertising his own
portrait on coins. These trends, let us repeat
it, appeared earlier than the Arab invasions,
and therefore cannot have been caused
directly and exclusively by them. Pepin
the Short was the first who tried to bring
back some uniformity in currency, and to
restore partially the regalian monopoly,
which the "rois fainéants" had allowed to
melt away. The easiest path towards uniformity obviously was to stress the existing

trends, and to suppress altogether the figured golden coins, relics of a dying past.
The political, artistic and economic renaissance under Charlemagne and Louis I was
incomplete and ephemeral; so was the
revival of figured and golden currency
during their reigns.

These observations take into no account
the possible influence of Arab invasions,
but do not exclude that there may have
been such an influence. However, we must
remark again a circumstance that Pirenne
and his followers seem to have overlooked:
the period of Arab conquest in the East,
and even in Spain, is not one of sudden
changes in the Merovingian currency.
Comparatively sweeping changes occurred
only when an autonomous dynasty took
power over Spain. This region had gold
currency under both the Visigoths and the
officers of the central Caliphate. But the
first independent Cordovan ruler, 'Abd al-
Rahmān I — *a contemporary of Pepin the
Short* — seems to have refrained both from
striking gold and from assuming the title
of Caliph, because another man ruled as
Caliph (although unlawfully) over the
Holy Cities of the Moslems. Only in the
tenth century, after the Eastern Caliphate
was practically dominated by the Turkish
guard, did 'Abd al-Rahmān III assume the
title of Caliph at Cordova. At the same
time, he began regularly to strike gold. It
is quite possible that the influence of the
silver standard in a neighbor state led Pepin
to carry out the complete abandonment of
the gold standard in his own kingdom.

Likewise, the example of the epigraphic
currency of the Arabs very likely encour-
aged Frankish moneyers to abandon entirely
the striking of figured coins, inasmuch as
these coins were struck mainly in Provence,
at the doorstep of Spain. This influence
could not be felt before the second quarter
of the eighth century, for in Spain the
Arabs did not suppress at once the figured
coins. To sum up, we may assume that *the
new trends in Frankish currency, begun
before the Arab conquests, were not influ-*

enced by the trade disruption that these conquests may have caused, but by parallel trends of Arab currency in Spain.

Islamic epigraphic currency not only influenced silver and copper coinage in the barbaric states of Western Europe, but even those gold coins, which had been regarded as the paramount show-place for the royal effigy. The only coins of this metal that Charlemagne struck in France (at Uzès, not far from the Arab border) are epigraphic. His contemporary, Offa, the Mercian king, struck gold with his name in Latin letters and a legend in Arabic, copied from an Abasside dīnār; even the date was that of the Hegira, 157 (774 A.D.). Imitations of this kind grew more and more abundant until the thirteenth century. Thus the Arab dīnār partly replaced the Byzantine nomisma as a model for the currency of Western Europe. Now this phenomenon is certainly not the symptom of a crisis in trade brought about by the Arabs; on the contrary, it shows that the Arab merchants for some time surpassed the Greeks.

Once more, the Lombard kingdom presented a different picture. While the Arabic states had no common borders with it, the Byzantine Empire enveloped it from almost every side, and even wedged into its central part. There was a continuous exchange of influences between the barbaric and the Byzantine mints of Italy; the mint of Ravenna passed from the Greeks to the Lombards a few months before Pepin began his work of restoration of state control on money in France. State control was never waived in the Lombard kingdom, and coinage remained faithful to the figured type, although, here too, artistic decadence caused legends to cover a larger and larger part of the coins. Furthermore, the predominance of the gold standard was never challenged; indeed, the quantity of silver in circulation seems to have been very scanty, as it was in the Empire. On the other hand, figured coins and the gold standard had remained paramount also in the Visigothic kingdom until it was conquered by the Arabs. Gold

emissions took place more than once in England from the time of Offa to that of Edward the Confessor. Thus we may conclude that *the new trends in Merovingian and early Carolingian currency were only local phenomena.*

It must be pointed out that Lombard gold coinage after Rothari did not bear the portrait of the Byzantine Emperor (except for the local currency of the dukes of Benevento), but that of the national king. Therefore, it constituted a challenge to the imperial regalian pretensions — the only challenge still existing since the Arabs and the Franks had adopted epigraphic types, and the Visigothic kingdom had been overrun. This challenge was not removed by Charlemagne when he conquered Italy. Lombard mints merely replaced on golden coins the portrait and the name of the national king with those of the new ruler. Meanwhile, in France, only epigraphic coinage was carried on as before. But there was a sudden change after Charlemagne was crowned emperor. Gold currency was discontinued all over his states, except for the epigraphic coins of Uzès, which were still in circulation in 813, despite some complaints of a council. The epigraphic currency of silver and copper was withdrawn, and replaced everywhere by coins of classic inspiration, bearing the portrait of the Emperor crowned with laurels, his name, and the imperial title.

There can be no doubt that the establishment of uniform standards for the whole empire was a step towards centralization. But it remains to be explained why the Byzantine figured type was chosen for silver and copper, and why such little gold as was still in circulation kept the epigraphic type. We are more likely to find a clue in Charlemagne's relations with the Byzantine Empire, than in the consequences of Arab invasions which occurred one century earlier or more! In fact, Charlemagne's assumption of the imperial title was certainly a hard blow to the Byzantine pretensions. Since the disappearance of the Sasanian and Aksumite monarchies, no foreign ruler had yet dared to style himself an Emperor. All the contemporary sources agree in pointing out that Charlemagne realized the gravity of his act. He made every possible effort to appease the Byzantine pride, and to secure some recognition of his title from the legitimate emperor of Constantinople. On the other hand, it has been remarked that he did not call himself "Romanorum imperator," like the Basileus, but "Imperator . . . Romanorum gubernans imperium." This title, being a little more modest than the other one, could possibly sound more acceptable to Constantinople than a formula implying absolute parity.

It may be suggested that the abandonment of figured gold currency, which removed the last challenge to the Byzantine monopoly, was another good-will move, intended to pave the way for an understanding. A similar arrangement had been worked out between Byzantium and Persia, and its memory had not been forgotten. Thus, in Italy, gold coinage was abandoned altogether, for it would have been difficult to persuade Italians to accept unusual non-figured coins. In France, epigraphic golden money was not a new thing; still, even there, it aroused complaints, apparently because it lent itself to forgery.

If our interpretation may be accepted, we shall infer that *Charlemagne's monetary reforms were not prompted by the progress of Arab invasions, but, primarily, by considerations of good-neighbor policy towards the Byzantine Empire.* Obviously this does not imply that the economic background had nothing to do with these reforms. Probably Charlemagne would not have sacrificed figured gold coinage to reconciliation with the Basileis unless the prestige and the economic usefulness of gold had already lost so much ground in France; to a large extent, his reforms were the completion of those of Pepin. But in Italy the economic situation did not justify the abandonment of gold. Since no new coins of this metal were produced at home after Charlemagne, foreign gold coins (Arabic

and Byzantine) took the place of the old Lombard currency all over the peninsula.

In 806, when the relations with the Eastern Empire were at their worst, Charlemagne did not even mention the imperial dignity in his division of his states among his sons. But an understanding, implying the recognition of Charlemagne as "imperator et basileus" by the Byzantine ambassadors, was finally reached in 812 at Aix-la-Chapelle. In the same place (not in Rome!), one year later, the old emperor placed the crown on the head of Louis the Pious and ordered him to be called "imperator et Augustus." In 814 Louis succeeded to the throne; he maintained passably good diplomatic relations with the Emperors of the East. The Basileis were drawn to a friendly attitude by their hope of securing the help of the second Carolingian "emperor" against the Arabs and the Bulgarians; but this hope was not realized. Much worse (at least, worse to the eyes of the ceremonial-conscious Byzantine Emperors), Louis felt bold enough to strike gold coins with his own name and portrait, of the same type as Charlemagne's imperial silver and copper. The obverse of these coins bore a crown with the words "minus divinum," implying that Louis was emperor by the grace of God, and not a sort of a cadet of his Eastern brother. It is true that this affirmation of power was not made from an Italian mint, even though Italy would have been the most appropriate soil on which to start gold currency again. The gold coinage of Louis was struck in that part of his empire which was the farthest from the Byzantine border, and the nearest to those uncivilized Germanic tribes which were still likely to be dazzled by the prestige of figured gold money. But, on their side, the Basileis Michael and Theophilus called themselves, in a letter to Louis, "in ipso Deo imperatores Romanorum." They branded him as "regi Francorum et Langobardorum et *vocato eorum* Imperatori!"

The ecclesiastic conflict for the parity of Constantinople with Rome, and for the Bulgarian church, gave the last blows to the crumbling compromise of Aix-la-Cha-pelle. When the balance of powers was definitely broken by the partition of the Western Empire, and by the accession of the energetic Macedonian dynasty in the East, Basil I formally withdrew the Byzantine recognition of the imperial rank of the Carolingian monarchs. Louis II could only send a diplomatic note, where he reminded Basil that, at any rate, the title of "basileus" had been granted in the past to many rulers —both heathen and Christians. But his protest remained unanswered. Under these circumstances, Louis II could well have retaliated by resuming gold currency. The princes of Benevento struck regularly gold money, and we know that for some years Louis II had silver struck in Benevento with his own name and imperial title. No golden coins of Louis have come down to us; but we cannot make much of a proof "ex silentio," since his power over Benevento lasted seven years only. Afterwards, Benevento recognized Byzantine overlordship; it is remarkable that no gold seems to have been struck there after this recognition.

At any rate, gold has always been essentially the instrument of international trade — as Marc Bloch has pointed out. For local trade silver was usually sufficient. Gold coins, if internationally accepted, were a vehicle of prestige for the ruler whose name and effigy they bore; but not every ruler's name could give international credit to golden coins. Already in the eighth century, the long intermission of gold coinage in France had caused Frankish money to disappear from those internationally accepted. Louis the Pious tried to go against the stream; but only the Frisians and the Saxons were impressed by his prestige enough to use widely his golden coins, and even to carry on for some time domestic imitations of them. But the powerless successors of Louis, who were not even able to maintain the sovereign monopoly of currency, could have no hope of persuading international merchants to carry along Frankish gold instead of the famous Byzantine *nomismata* and Moslem *dīnār*. In conclusion, *the*

definitive abandonment of the gold standard after Louis the Pious was not directly connected with the Arab invasions, but depended on the insufficient prestige of the Western monarchs. Only when the prestige of both the Greeks and Arabs declined, in the thirteenth century was it possible to resume the striking of gold in Western Europe.

If neither the "disappearance" of papyrus nor that of gold currency is connected with a sudden regression in trade caused by the Arab conquests, the thesis of Pirenne has little support left. As a matter of fact, the evidence collected in the above-mentioned essay of Sabbe is more than sufficient to prove that the trade of Oriental purple-dyed and embroidered cloths was never interrupted in Western Europe. At the most, we can suppose that this trade suffered a temporary depression — although there are no grounds for this supposition, and, at any rate, no comparative statistics can be drawn when sources are casual, scant, and far between. Nevertheless, for the sake of a further demonstration, we shall assume that there was a depression. Must such a hypothetical trend be connected with a general disruption of trade?

First of all, we should take into account the trends in matters of etiquette and costumes. Let us repeat that the value of a symbol does not reach farther than the convention on which the symbol is based. A flag would have been a scrap of cloth in the Roman Republic. The Huns and most of the early Germans did not care for imperial purple. Now we may agree with Halphen in discounting as a sheer invention the witty anecdote of the Monk of Saint Gall, where Charlemagne is shown playing a cunning trick on his officers, who had preferred refined Oriental garments to the simple national costumes. Still the anecdote is doubtless evidence of a widespread attitude of the Franks when the Monk was writing, in the second half of the ninth century. Another source relates that Charles the Bald, after being crowned by John III, wore a Byzantine ceremonial dress, and drew upon himself the blame of his subjects for spurning "the tradition of the Frankish kings for the Greek vanity." Again the source is unfair to Charles — although the "Hellenism" of this sovereign, expecially in regalian matters, is an undoubted fact. But the ground chosen to put blame on Charles must express an actual sentiment.

In conclusion, *the diminished use of Oriental cloths among the laymen* (if there was a diminution) *depended to a great extent on a change in fashions. The Church did not change fashions,* and, in fact, *the largest part of the existing evidence of Oriental cloths in Western Europe relates to the Church.*

On the other hand, we must remember that the regalian monopoly of cloths and jewelry — unlike the monopolies of currency and papyrus — did not cover only manufacturing and trade, but the use itself of many qualities of these objects. The expressions of the Byzantine "kommerkiarioi" (customs-officers), as related by Liudprand[6] in the tenth century, are significant. The Greeks maintained that the wearing of cloths dyed with special qualities of purple (including some which were not reserved to the emperor and to the high officers) should be allowed only to the Byzantine nation, "as we surpass all other nations in wealth and wisdom." Thus the monopoly of cloths, like that of gold currency, had ceased to be an arbitrary imposition of the government, and had taken roots in popular feelings.

A very meticulous and complex set of provisions (which we know in detail only for the tenth century, but based to a large extent on laws of the late Roman Empire) established various categories of cloths, according to qualities of dye and to size. Some categories could be exported without restrictions, some were vetoed to exporters, some could be purchased only in limited amounts. Subjects of the Empire (such as the Venetians and the citizens of some Southern Italian cities) and merchants of some allied countries (such as Bulgarians and Russians) enjoyed special facilities by treaty. But in no case was unlimited exportation granted. Even churches and monasteries, if located in foreign countries, could not get Byzantine ceremonial objects for their shrines without special permission by the Basileus. Foreign ambassadors had to submit their luggage to the visit of the "kommerkiarioi," whose final inspection completed the usual, permanent control of the cloth market and of the jewelry-shops entrusted to special city officers.

Under these circumstances, the largest source of supply for Western Europe probably was the already mentioned custom of the Emperors of sending ceremonial objects as diplomatic gifts. Some Emperors dispensed such gifts lavishly both to foreign princes and to churches. But those monarchs who felt little necessity to win over allies or to conciliate the Western Church — for instance, the great Iconoclasts, contemporary of Charles Martel and Pepin the Short — were much stricter. As late as the tenth century, Constantinus Porphyrogenitus warned his son against complying with the requests for imperial crowns, stoles and cloths, which were so frequently advanced by the Mongolic and Slavonic neighbors of the Empire. These stoles and crowns, he said (and he almost believed it) were not made by human hands, but sent from Heaven by the Angels themselves.

To be sure, there was another source of supply: smuggling. Vigilant and numerous as they were, the controllers could not see everything; and they were only too often bribable at will. If we should believe the unfair account of Liudprand, at the time of Constantine Porphyrogenitus even the prostitutes in Italy could bestow on themselves the very ornaments which the Angels had intended for the august Basileus only. But Liudprand grossly exaggerates. The price itself of Oriental cloths, the cost of transportation, and the bribe for the com-

[6] Liudprand (ca. 922–972), Bishop of Cremona and an important historian. The work here cited is an account of his mission (for Otto I) to Constantinople in 968. [Editor's note]

plaisant officers must have reserved to very few Westerners the pleasure of bootlegged goods, even under as weak an emperor as Constantine VII. When the power was in the hands of a man "tachucheir," with a long reach (such as Nicephorus Phocas), smuggling must have been practically impossible.

However, Oriental cloths could be purchased in Arabic-ruled countries, too. It is true that since 'Abd al-Malik a monopoly had been established, and that Moslem rulers, in general, were more sparing than the Basileis in their diplomatic gifts of cloths. But, as a rule, the restrictions enforced by Islamic princes were not as tight as those of the Eastern Empire. This explains why many great personages of Western Europe — including clergymen and crusaders — displayed on many occasions glowing ceremonial garments, where the praise of Allah was embroidered in the "tirāz," in words luckily unintelligible to most of the bearers of such a cloth!

To sum up, *any fluctuation which may be noticed in the supply of Oriental cloths is likely to stem from a fluctuation in the efficiency of state control or in the system of alliances of the Byzantine and Arab governments. The rise of the Arab Empire, far from curtailing supply, made it a little less difficult to obtain cloth, because of the Arabs' looser notion of regalian monopoly.*

Of fluctuations in the trade of spices we know but little. Some of the documents quoted by Sabbe show that spices too were occasionally imported into Western Europe, right at the time when Pirenne speaks of disappearance. But, unfortunately, we have no specific essay on that question. I shall give only a few general remarks, which are a suggestion of fields for investigation, rather than matter-of-fact statements.

Once more, the evolution of taste should be taken into account. Were the tough noblemen and the rough ecclesiastic grandees of early medieval Western Europe as fond of spiced food as the Romans and the men of the Renaissance? We know that the latter were persons of a nice palate. The gastronomic history of the early Middle Ages has not been expounded as yet in detail, but the hypothesis of a coarser taste may be not altogether unlikely.

On the other hand, the spices arrived from countries so different and far apart, that it is not enough to connect the fluctuations in supply with the general relations between the Arab world and Western Europe. Revolutions which occurred in the Asiatic Far East, or in Dark Africa, may have affected the spice trade very deeply. In 1343, according to an Italian chronicler, a war between the Golden Horde and the Genoese colonies in Crimea caused spices to rise from fifty to one hundred per cent in price. It should be expected that crises of the same kind were caused by Asiatic wars of the early Middle Ages. Now the eighth century, which saw the rise of the Carolingians in Western Europe, was an epoch of troubles for Eastern Asia. India was going through the crisis which followed the defeat of Buddhism and the triumph of Rajput "feudalism." While the Arabs invaded the Sindh in 712, Hindustan was being split into a great number of petty states. The Chinese T'ang dynasty, after reaching the peak of its power in the seventh century, suffered severe blows. In 751 the Arabs stopped the Chinese expansion in Central Asia (battle of Talas). Between 755 and 763 the emperors, driven out of their capital by a revolution, asked the help of the Uighurs to retake the city — a remedy worse than the sore. In 758, the Moslems sacked and burned Canton. These do not seem very favorable circumstances for the continuity of trade relations. But the situation gradually improved in the ninth century, and, in fact, evidence of spices in Western Europe grows less scant in that century.

EAST AND WEST IN THE EARLY MIDDLE AGES

ROBERT S. LOPEZ

THE SECOND POINT we have to investigate is the problem of continuity. Granted that alternations of better and worse periods are unavoidable in any protracted economic activity, and that large scale commerce in early mediaeval Catholic Europe cannot be expected at any period, can we assume that commercial relations with the Byzantine and Muslim world were never interrupted, or do we have to look for a total eclipse at a certain moment?

For the fifth, sixth, and early seventh centuries the question does not arise. Virtually nobody believes any more that the barbarian invasions of the fifth century marked a sharp turn in economic history, although most historians will admit that the meeting of German immaturity with Roman decrepitude accelerated the process of disintegration whose first symptoms can be traced as far back as the age of the Antonines. The sixth century culminated in the partial restoration of Mediterranean unity under Byzantine auspices. Astride that century and the following one the letters of Gregory I give us a full documentation of continuing, if thinned out, intercourse between the Mediterranean East and virtually all parts of Europe. Under Justinian, China had unwittingly made its earliest contribution to the economic equipment of Europe — the silkworm — and in the time of Heraclius[1] Egyptian ships again crossed the strait of Gibraltar to obtain English tin. Slowly but steadily, the Western barbarians rebuilt a network of communications with one another, ultimately leading to the more refined East. Countries which in antiquity had been almost untouched by Rome, such as Ireland and the Baltic regions, now began to look toward Constantinople. What commerce has lost in intensity was partly compensated for by gains in geographic expansion.

Paradoxically, the absolution of the backward Germans paved the way for an indictment of the progressive Arabs. While some scholars were content with mild accusations and roundabout charges — the Arabs weakened the international trade of the Mediterranean by moving the economic center of gravity eastwards to Irak and Persia, or by touching off a Byzantine reprisal blockade across the traditional sea routes — Henri Pirenne made the Arabs squarely and directly responsible for pulling an iron curtain which separated the Believers from the Infidels and left Europe an economic and cultural dead end. His superb pleading and his personal charm won many converts. Nevertheless, a large number of scholars — the majority, I should say — were not convinced. For the last twenty years nearly all that has been written on early mediaeval economic history has reflected the heat of the controversy on "les thèses d'Henri Pirenne." Probably the law of diminishing returns should persuade us to move on to equally controversial and less belabored fields. This does not exempt us, however, from recalling briefly the main issues. Inasmuch as I have long been an admirer of

[1] Heraclius, a Byzantine Emperor, 610–641. [Editor's note]

From R. S. Lopez, "East and West in the Early Middle Ages: Economic Relations." Paper read in 1955 at Tenth International Congress of Historical Sciences, convening in Rome. Printed in *Relazioni del X Congresso Internazionale di Scienze Storiche*, vol. III, pp. 129–137. G. C. Sansoni — Editore, Firenze. Reprinted by permission of G. C. Sansoni and Professor Lopez.

Pirenne but an opponent of "Mahomet et Charlemagne," I shall not pretend impartiality.

It has been argued that Arab regular fleets and piratical parties made the Mediterranean impassable for Christian ships at one time or another. For short intervals and in specific areas, this is an undeniable fact. To the many instances cited by Pirenne and his followers I would like to add a testimony they overlooked: the Life of St. Gregory Decapolites (780–842). It describes the Byzantine ships and sailors of Ephesus as bottled up in the port for fear of Islamic pirates, a ship of Enos as chased along a river by Slavic pirates, and navigation from Corinth to Rome as extremely dangerous on account of Sicilian pirates. Still it is obvious that pirates could not have multiplied and survived without trade to prey upon. There always were calmer interludes and fairly safe detours; and even the worst hurdles could be leaped over by fast blockade runners or smashed through by heavily protected convoys. To be sure, all of this made the high cost of transportation still higher; but the cost was not the main consideration in the international trade of the early middle ages, which both before and after the coming of the Arabs consisted above all of luxury wares and war materials. At any rate, war hazards are far from incompatible with commercial expansion and trade in cheaper goods. In the thirteenth century both war risks and the volume of trade in the Mediterranean world grew to unprecedented amounts.

It has been claimed, openly or by implication, that the conflict between Muslims and Christians differed from other collisions in the Mediterranean because it was an "antagonism between two creeds" or, indeed, between "two worlds mutually foreign and hostile." Even on theoretical grounds, this contention is questionable. Their paths diverged more and more with time, but originally both the Arabs and the Germans were wanderers who adopted Greco-Roman institutions and Hebraic monotheism. In the eyes of Christian theologians, Moham-med was a heretic, not a pagan; in the words of Muslim lawyers, the Christians were a "people of the Book," not heathens who ought to be either converted or killed. Of course there was mutual hatred and name calling, though probably not as much as during and after the Crusades; but hatred does not occur solely between peoples of a different creed. It certainly did not prevent political and economic intercourse. To cite only a few illustrations from the Carolingian period, in 813 the ambassadors of the Aghlabid[2] emir aboard a Venetian convoy aided the Christian crew in attacking a convoy of Spanish Muslims. Then they proceeded to Sicily, to renew with the Byzantine governor the agreement which ensured to the citizens of each country the right to travel and trade in the other. A few years later, the Bishop and Duke of Naples — a Christian port which had welcomed Muslim ships as early as 722 — joined the rulers of Amalfi and Gaeta in an alliance with the Muslims against Pope John VIII. The alliance was so profitable that the Pope was unable to win back the support of Amalfi either by threatening excommunication or by offering total customs exemption in Rome and a subsidy of no less than 10,000 silver *mancusi* a year. Ironically, the *mancusi* in all probability were Islamic coins, and the papyrus used by the Pope for his diplomatic campaign was made in Egypt and bore at its top an Arab inscription praising Allah. Should one suggest that the capital of Christianity was too near the Islamic border to be typical of Christian attitudes, we might recall the friendship of Charlemagne and Mohammed's Successor, Harun al-Rashid.[3] It resulted not only in the foundation of an inn for pilgrims in Jerusalem, but also in the establishment of a market across the street, where the pilgrims

2 The Aghlabids were a ninth century dynasty in Africa which became virtually independent. [Editor's note]

3 Harun al-Rashid (ca. 764–809) was the most famous of the Abbasid caliphs and a patron of arts and letters under whom Bagdad reached its height. [Editor's note]

by paying two dinars a year could carry on their business.

Indirect proofs of the purportedly catastrophic effects of the Arab expansion have been sought for in a supposed aggravation of the general symptoms of economic and intellectual depression in Catholic Europe. We cannot discuss these symptoms without changing our theme to a general investigation of early mediaeval economy and culture. Personally, I do not believe that the depression was more acute in the Carolingian than in the Merovingian period. The earlier centuries of the early middle ages benefited from the fact that Roman roads and towns, institutions and traditions had not entirely disintegrated, and that disheartened Roman personnel still lent a hand to inexperienced barbarians. The later centuries benefited from the fact that the further shrinking of the legacy of antiquity forced the new world to make its first clumsy attempts at reorganizing roads, towns, institutions and traditions with a personnel of mixed blood and rudimental training. Whether this pale dawn was better or worse than the previous pale dusk is anybody's guess: judgments on cultural achievements depend largely on personal taste, and exact economic comparisons between two adjoining and similar periods cannot be made without some statistical base. But even if Carolingian inferiority were ascertainable it could not be pinned *a priori* on the impact of Arab invasions rather than on the lingering inability of the West to reverse an old downward trend.

It would be still more rash to draw general inferences from ascertained changes of a limited scope. The fact that during the Carolingian period the ports of Provence and Languedoc lost trade to those of northeastern and southwestern Italy, or that Syrian and Greek merchants in the West yielded their prominence to Jews and Scandinavians does not by itself prove a breakdown of Mediterranean commerce any more than the displacement of Seville and Lisbon by Antwerp and Amsterdam in the early modern age denotes a collapse of Atlantic trade. The passing of economy primacy from one people to another is a normal trait of the historical process. Again, the decrease and cessation of the imports of Palestinian wine, Egyptian papyrus and (to a lesser extent) some other Oriental commodities does not necessarily stem from general difficulties in trade. Specific changes in taste, fashions, traditions, and methods of production may be responsible for a wane in the demand or the offer of individual wares. To all this I shall return very soon; here a passing mention of the problem will be sufficient.

We still have to consider the possibility that trade between East and West came to a virtual end not because of the Arab invasions but owing to the gradual exhaustion of the gold and silver stocks of Catholic Europe. The problem has been studied by some of the greatest historians of the last generation — Marc Bloch and Michael Rostovtzeff among others — but it is still obscure: monetary phenomena always are hard to interpret, and for the early middle ages information is desperately scant. We do know that the later Roman emperors already expressed alarm at the double drainage of currency through private hoarding and the export of coins or bullion to Persia, India, and China in exchange for luxury goods. To be sure, mercantilistic instincts and traditional dislike for extravagant expenditure and foreign manners may have added emphasis to their words; moreover, they found greedy hoarders and selfish merchants good scapegoats to share the blame for inflation, taxation and economic misery. Still, there is archaeologic confirmation of their claims — hoards within the empire and Roman coins scattered through Asia. The Byzantine Empire made conservation of its stocks of precious metals a cardinal point of its economic policies. The stockpile had ups and downs, but in the early middle ages it never was depleted so much that it was not possible to maintain a stable and fairly abundant currency in gold, silver and copper. The Islamic countries were blessed with sensational discoveries of gold and silver mines. Catholic Europe, however, fell heir to the poorer half of the formerly Roman territory, which had no rich mines and no thriving trades. Hoarding was carried out in abnormally high proportions. Coinage declined in quality and quantity until the only local currency consisted of puny silver deniers struck in modest amounts. Could this not be an indication that Catholic Europe had practically used up its precious metals and no longer had the means to pay for imports from the East?

The answer is not as simple as one might think at first. Probably Catholic Europe would have been unable to carry out large purchases in the Byzantine and Muslim markets with the small amount of coinage it struck and maintained in circulation, or with the Byzantine and Muslim coins that war or trade channeled to its coffers. But there is no reason to assume that Catholic Europe desired to purchase more goods than it could easily afford. Remarkably, the lay and ecclesiastic lords who were the best potential customers of Eastern luxury goods also were the greatest hoarders. Their unspent and cumbersome wealth lay frozen in bars, rings, jewels, and other artistic objects. From the tenth century on, when the revival of trade and culture caused the demand for Eastern goods to skyrocket, those treasures were melted down; nothing would have prevented their owners from melting them sooner if they had needed cash. Quite to the contrary, what evidence we have conveys the impression that hoards grew in size during the eighth and ninth centuries.

There is no direct way to calculate the balance of payments in the trade of Catholic Europe with the Byzantine and Muslim East, but all that we know about the vast economic and cultural gulf which separated these worlds and about the goods which were prevalent in the exchanges between them enables us to venture a guess. In all probability early mediaeval Europe, with its rude society of affluent lords and penniless peasants, behaved towards the refined and complex societies of Byzantium and Islam like any other backward country that does not crave for many outlandish manufactured goods and has an excess of raw materials available for export. Ordinarily in such cases the balance of payments is favorable to the backward country. The more advanced nations have to offset their commercial deficit by remitting gold and silver, unless they are ready to tip the scales with the sword and impose upon the "inferior" or "infidel" race some sort of tributary or colonial regime. The latter method was not unknown in the early middle ages; Byzantine fiscality and Arab raids often extorted from one or another underdeveloped and weak European country many goods for which no adequate payment was offered. But the Venetians and the Vikings, the Franks and the Jews were too strong or too crafty to yield to sheer force. They must have been paid good cash.

Any guess is open to challenge. Let us assume that our guess was wrong, and that Catholic Europe for a few centuries or for the whole duration of the early middle ages exported cash to pay for the Oriental commodities it wanted to import; would this force us to postulate that its stock of precious metals was eventually exhausted? I do not believe it would. The quantities involved were so small that the local production of gold and silver was more than enough to meet the current demand without drawing from the reserve. A certain amount of silver, it is true, had to be set aside for the striking of deniers; gold, however, was not used by Western mints except for occasional emissions of ceremonial coins or for imitations of Byzantine and Islamic coins. The rest was available for hoarding, adornment and foreign trade. The same princes and prelates who handed out so much gold to smiths in order to have goblets and reliquaries could well deliver gold to merchants in exchange for Oriental spices and perfumes. Their purchases would have sufficed to keep trade with the East going — a small trickle, perhaps, but a stirring, incessant reminder to provincial and countrified Europe that there were other worlds with a quicker, broader and richer way of life.

Eventually not economic stagnation, but economic growth made the monetary stock of Europe inadequate. In the tenth century the laborious search for gold in the Italian, French and German rivers was intensified, and the discovery of rich silver mines near Goslar[4] started a "silver rush" of consider-

4 Goslar is in central Germany, at the northern edge of the Harz Mountains. [Editor's note]

able proportions. Yet we have good reasons to believe that the exports of Catholic Europe to the Eastern world were increasing. We have to use the richer evidence of the tenth century to supplement that of earlier centuries on which so little is known, but we ought to remember that a new era was already in the making, and that early mediaeval stagnation was about to yield to the Commercial Revolution of the later middle ages.

TECHNOLOGY AND INVENTION IN
THE MIDDLE AGES

LYNN WHITE, JR.

Educated at Stanford and Harvard, Lynn White, Jr., taught history
at Princeton and Stanford before becoming president of Mills College
in 1943. As a historian one of his areas of research has been the badly
neglected field of medieval technology; the article, excerpted below,
received wide attention. Dr. White was interested not so much in ques-
tioning the Pirenne Thesis as in suggesting that in agricultural improvements there is a parallel explanation for the transference of European
Civilization from the Mediterranean to the North.

THE HISTORY of technology and invention, especially that of the earlier
periods, has been left strangely unculti-
vated. Our vast technical institutes continue
at an ever-accelerating pace to revolutionize
the world we live in; yet small effort is
being made to place our present technology
in the time-sequence, or to give to our
technicians that sense of their social responsibility which can only come from an exact
understanding of their historical function
— one might almost say, of their apostolic
succession. By permitting those who work
in shops and laboratories to forget the past,
we have impoverished the present and en-
dangered the future. In the United States
this neglect is the less excusable because we
Americans boast of being the most technically progressive people of an inventive age.
But when the historian of American technology tries to probe the medieval and
renaissance roots of his subject he runs into
difficulties: the materials available to him
are scanty and often questionable; for professional mediaevalists have left unmined
this vein in the centuries on which they
have staked their claim. . . .

Perhaps the chief reason why scholars
have been hesitant to explore the subject is
the difficulty of delimiting its boundaries:
technology knows neither chronological nor
geographic frontiers.

The student of the history of invention
soon discovers that he must smash the conventional barriers between Greek and barbarian, Roman and German, oriental and
occidental. For mediaeval technology is
found to consist not simply of the technical
equipment inherited from the Roman-
Hellenistic world modified by the inventive
ingenuity of the western peoples, but also
of elements derived from three outside
sources: the northern barbarians, the Byzantine and Moslem Near East, and the
Far East.

The importance of the first of these, the
barbarian influence, has been far too little
understood even by those who have dabbled
in the history of technology. Students of
the fine arts have only recently led the way
towards an appreciation of the essential
unity and originality of that vast northern
world of so-called "barbarians" which, in
ancient times, had its focal point on the

From Lynn White, Jr., "Technology and Invention in the Middle Ages," *Speculum*, XV (April 1940),
pp. 141, 143–144, 149–150, 151–156. By permission of The Medieval Academy of America, Cambridge, Mass.

plains of Russia and of Western Siberia, but which extended from the Altai Mountains to Ireland: we are beginning to learn how profoundly it affected the aesthetic expressions of the Middle Ages. But even before the Germanic migrations, these barbarians had begun to influence Roman technology, and in later centuries they contributed many distinctive ingredients to mediaeval life: trousers and the habit of wearing furs, the easily-heated compact house as contrasted with the Mediterranean patio-house, cloisonné jewelry, feltmaking, the ski, the use of soap for cleansing, and of butter in place of olive oil, the making of barrels and tubs, the cultivation of rye, oats, spelt, and hops, perhaps the sport of falconry and certain elements of the number-system. Above all, the great plains invented the stirrup, which made the horse etymologically responsible for chivalry, and, perhaps even more important, the heavy plow which, as we shall see, is the technological basis of the typical mediaeval manor. . . .

The student of European technics, then, is compelled to follow his subject far beyond the usual geographical limits of mediaeval research. Similarly he finds that for his purposes the customary tripartite division of history into ancient, mediaeval and modern is completely arbitrary. In particular he finds no evidence of a break in the continuity of technological development following the decline of the Western Roman Empire.

The Dark Ages doubtless deserve their name: political disintegration, economic depression, the debasement of religion and the collapse of literature surely made the barbarian kingdoms in some ways unimaginably dismal. Yet because many aspects of civilization were in decay we should not assume too quickly that everything was back-sliding. Even an apparent coarsening may indicate merely a shift of interest: in modern painting we recognize that Van Gogh's technical methods were not those of David; so, when we contrast a Hellenistic carved gem with a Merovingian enamel,

our judgment should be cautious. Few will dispute that the Irish illumination and the Scandinavian jewelry of the seventh and eighth centuries stand among the supreme arts of all time; yet they are far from classical canons of taste, being rooted in an ancient, and quite separate, tradition of Northern art. So in the history of technology we must be discriminating. Changing tastes and conditions may lead to the degeneration of one technique while the technology of the age as a whole is advancing. The technology of torture, for example, which achieved such hair-raising perfection during the Renaissance, is now happily in eclipse: viewed historically, our modern American "third degree" is barbaric only in its simplicity.

Indeed, a dark age may stimulate rather than hinder technology. Economic catastrophe in the United States during the past decade has done nothing to halt invention — quite the contrary; and it is a commonplace that war encourages technological advance. Confusion and depression, which bring havoc in so many areas of life, may have just the opposite effect on technics. And the chances of this are particularly good in a period of general migration, when peoples of diverse backgrounds and inheritances are mixing.

There is, in fact, no proof that any important skills of the Graeco-Roman world were lost during the Dark Ages even in the unenlightened West, much less in the flourishing Byzantine and Saracenic Orient. To be sure, the diminished wealth and power of the Germanic kings made engineering on the old Roman scale infrequent; yet the full technology of antiquity was available when required: the 276-ton monolith which crowns the tomb of Theodoric the Ostrogoth was brought to Ravenna from Istria; while more than two centuries later Charlemagne transported not only sizable columns but even a great equestrian statue of Zeno from Ravenna across the Alps to Aachen. Incidentally, we should do well to remember that the northern peoples from remote times were capable of managing great weights, as witness Stonehenge and the dolmens. . . .

Indeed, the technical skill of classical times was not simply maintained: it was considerably improved. Our view of history has been too top-lofty. We have been dazzled by aspects of civilization which are in every age the property of an élite, and in which the common man, with rare exceptions, has had little part. The so-called "higher" realms of culture might decay, government might fall into anarchy, and trade be reduced to a trickle, but through it all, in the fact of turmoil and hard times, the peasant and artisan carried on, and even improved their lot. In technology, at least, the Dark Ages mark a steady and uninterrupted advance over the Roman Empire. Evidence is accumulating to show that a serf in the turbulent and insecure tenth century enjoyed a standard of living considerably higher than that of a proletarian in the reign of Augustus.

The basic occupation was, of course, agriculture. We have passed through at least two agricultural revolutions: that which began with "Turnip" Townshend and Jethro Tull in the early eighteenth century, and another, equally important, in the Dark Ages.

The problem of the development and diffusion of the northern wheeled plow, equipped with colter, horizontal share and moldboard, is too thorny to be discussed here. Experts seem generally agreed: (1) that the new plow greatly increased production by making possible the tillage of rich, heavy, badly-drained river-bottom soils; (2) that it saved labor by making cross-plowing superfluous, and thus produced the typical northern strip-system of land division, as distinct from the older block-system dictated by the cross-plowing necessary with the lighter Mediterranean plow; (3) most important of all, that the heavy plow needed such power that peasants pooled their oxen and plowed together, thus laying the basis for the mediaeval coöperative agricultural community, the manor. But whatever may be the date and origin of the fully developed heavy plow, its effects were supplemented and greatly enhanced in the later eighth century by the invention of the three-field system, an improved rotation of crops and fallow which greatly increased the efficiency of agricultural labor. For example, by switching 600 acres from the two-field to the three-field system, a community of peasants could plant 100 acres more in crops each year with 100 acres less of plowing. Since fallow land was plowed twice to keep down the weeds, the old plan required three acres of plowing for every acre in crops, whereas the new plan required only two acres of plowing for every productive acre.

In a society overwhelmingly agrarian, the result of such an innovation could be nothing less than revolutionary. Pirenne is only the most recent of many historians to speculate as to why the reign of Charlemagne witnessed the shift of the center of European civilization, the change of the focus of history, from the Mediterranean to the plains of Northern Europe. The findings of agricultural history, it seems, have never been applied to this central problem in the study of the growth of the northern races. Since the spring sowing, which was the chief novelty of the three-field system, was unprofitable in the south because of the scarcity of summer rains, the three-field system did not spread below the Alps and Loire. For obvious reasons of climate the agricultural revolution of the eighth century was confined to Northern Europe. It would appear, therefore, that it was this more efficient and productive use of land and labor which gave to the northern plains an economic advantage over the Mediterranean shores, and which, from Charlemagne's time onward, enabled the Northern Europeans in short order to surpass both in prosperity and in culture the peoples of an older inheritance.

In ways less immediately significant the Dark Ages likewise made ingenious improvements. One of the most important of these was a contribution to practical mechanics. There are two basic forms of motion: reciprocal and rotary. The normal device for connecting these — a device without which our machine civilization is inconceivable— is the crank. The crank is an invention second in importance only to the wheel itself; yet the crank was unknown to the Greeks and the Romans. It appears, even in rudimentary form, only after the Invasions: first, perhaps, in hand-querns, then on rotary grindstones. The later Middle Ages developed its application to all sorts of machinery.

Clearly there are nuggets in this stream for anyone to find. Perhaps the most successful amateur student of early mediaeval technology was the Commandant Lefebvre des Noëttes, who after his retirement from active service in the French cavalry, devoted himself to his hobby, the history of horses. He died in 1936, having made discoveries which must greatly modify our judgment of the Carolingian period. From his investigations Lefebvre des Noëttes concluded that the use of animal power in antiquity was unbelievably inefficient. The ancients did not use nailed shoes on their animals, and broken hooves often rendered beasts useless. Besides, they knew only the yoke-system of harness. While this was adequate for oxen, it was most unsatisfactory for the more rapid horse. The yoke rested on the withers of a team. From each end of the yoke ran two flexible straps: one a girth behind the forelegs, the other circling the horse's neck. As soon as the horse began to pull, the flexible front strap pressed on his windpipe, and the harder he pulled the closer he came to strangulation. Moreover the ancient harness was mechanically defective: the yoke was too high to permit the horse to exert his full force in pulling by flinging his body-weight into the task. Finally, the ancients were unable to harness one animal in front of another. Thus all great weights had to be drawn by gangs of slaves, since animal power was not technically available in sufficient quantities.

According to Lefebvre des Noëttes this condition remained unchanged until the later ninth or early tenth century when,

almost simultaneously, three major inventions appear: the modern horse-collar, the tandem harness, and the horseshoe. The modern harness, consisting of a rigid horse-collar resting on the shoulders of the beast, permitted him to breathe freely. This was connected to the load by lateral traces which enabled the horse to throw his whole body into pulling. It has been shown experimentally that this new apparatus so greatly increased the effective animal power that a team which can pull only about one thousand pounds with the antique yoke can pull three or four times that weight when equipped with the new harness. Equally important was the extension of the traces so that tandem harnessing was possible, thus providing an indefinite amount of animal power for the transport of great weights. Finally, the introduction of the nailed horseshoe improved traction and greatly increased the endurance of the newly available animal power. Taken together these three inventions suddenly gave Europe a new supply of non-human power, at no increase of expense or labor. They did for the eleventh and twelfth centuries what the steam-engine did for the nineteenth. Lefebvre des Noëttes has therefore offered an unexpected and plausible solution for the most puzzling problem of the Middle Ages: the sudden upswing of European vitality after the year 1000.

However, Lefebvre des Noëttes failed to point out the relation between this access of energy and the contemporary agricultural revolution. He noted that the new harness made the horse available for agricultural labor: the first picture of a horse so engaged is found in the Bayeux Tapestry. But while the horse is a rapid and efficient power engine, it burns an expensive fuel — grain — as compared with the slower, but cheaper, hay-burning ox. Under the two-field system the peasants' margin of production was insufficient to support a work-horse; under the three-field system the horse gradually displaced the ox as the normal plow and draft animal of the northern plains. By the later Middle Ages there is a clear correlation on the one hand between the horse and the three-field system and on the other between the ox and the two-field system. The contrast is essentially one between the standards of living and of labor-productivity of the northern and the southern peasantry: the ox saves food; the horse saves man-hours. The new agriculture, therefore, enabled the north to exploit the new power more effectively than the Mediterranean regions could, and thereby the northerners increased their prosperity still further.

Naturally Lefebvre des Noëttes made mistakes: only when his work receives the recognition it deserves will these be rectified. His use of the monuments is not impeccable; his almost exclusive concern with pictures led him to neglect the texts, particularly Pliny's assertion that at times Italian peasants (presumably in the Po valley) plowed with several yokes of oxen; and he overlooks the complex question of the eight-ox plow-team as a basis for land division in pre-Carolingian times. Moreover an etymologist has recently shown that the word for "horse-collar" in the Teutonic and Slavic tongues (English: hames) is derived from Central-Asiatic sources, implying a diffusion of the modern harness westward from the nomadic steppe-culture. Doubtless criticism will eventually show that Lefebvre des Noëttes' three inventions developed rather more slowly than he thought. But that they grew and spread during the Dark Ages, and that they profoundly affected European society, seems already proved. . . .

The cumulative effect of the newly available animal, water, and wind power upon the culture of Europe has not been carefully studied. But from the twelfth and even from the eleventh, century there was a rapid replacement of human by non-human energy wherever great quantities of power were needed or where the required motion was so simple and monotonous that a man could be replaced by a mechanism. The chief glory of the later Middle Ages was not its cathedrals or its epics or its scholasticism: it was the building for the first time in history of a complex civilization which rested not on the backs of sweating slaves or coolies but primarily on non-human power.

The study of mediaeval technology is therefore far more than an aspect of economic history: it reveals a chapter in the conquest of freedom. More than that, it is a part of the history of religion. The humanitarian technology which our modern world has inherited from the Middle Ages was not rooted in economic necessity; for this "necessity" is inherent in every society, yet has found inventive expression only in the Occident, nurtured in the activist or voluntarist tradition of Western theology. It is ideas which make necessity conscious. The labor-saving power-machines of the later Middle Ages were produced by the implicit theological assumption of the infinite worth of even the most degraded human personality, by an instinctive repugnance towards subjecting any man to a monotonous drudgery which seems less than human in that it requires the exercise neither of intelligence nor of choice. It has often been remarked that the Latin Middle Ages first discovered the dignity and spiritual value of labor — that to labor is to pray. But the Middle Ages went further: they gradually and very slowly began to explore the practical implications of an essentially Christian paradox: that just as the Heavenly Jerusalem contains no temple, so the goal of labor is to end labor.

PIRENNE AND MUHAMMAD

DANIEL C. DENNETT, JR.

Editorial note attached to the article in *Speculum:* "The author of this article was killed when the plane in which he was travelling on government service crashed over Ethiopia on 22 March 1947. An able scholar, expert in the languages and history of the Near East, Dr. Dennett had served as instructor in history at Harvard previous to his appointment in 1942 as Cultural Relations Attaché at the American Legation in Beirut, a post he held until his untimely death at the age of thirty-seven."

HENRI PIRENNE summarized the results of a distinguished career in his last work, *Mohammed and Charlemagne* (New York, 1939), published posthumously by his executors and unfortunately without revision by author. In this book, which restates without appreciable alteration, despite wide and sometimes bitter controversy, the conclusions reached in a series of well-known articles, the author sets forth the following thesis:

Because the Germanic invaders had neither the desire, nor the unity of purpose, to destroy the Roman Empire, "Romania" existed as both concept and fact for more than two centuries after 476. The Emperor had abdicated nothing of his universal sovereignty and the barbarian rulers of the West acknowledged his primacy. Thus "the Empire subsisted, in law, as a sort of mystical presence; in fact — and this is much more important — it was 'Romania' that survived." Inasmuch as the invaders represented a bare five per cent of the population, they were Romanized. The language of Gaul was Latin, the system of government and administration remained unchanged, Roman law still survived, the Empire was the only world power and its foreign policy embraced all Europe, with the result that the only positive element in history was the influence of the Empire which "continued to be Roman, just as the United States of North America, despite immigration, have remained Anglo Saxon."

The best proof of the persistence of Romania is to be found in the flourishing commerce of Gaul to which Syrian traders on the free Mediterranean brought the spices of the Orient, the wines of Gaza, the papyrus of Egypt, and the oil of North Africa. This commerce played a crucial role in the economic, social, and political life of Gaul, which was chiefly supported by its influence. Nor was it small commerce, since "I think we may say that navigation was at least as active as under the Empire." Because of it, the monetary system of the barbarians was that of Rome, and the currency was gold in contrast to the system of silver monometallism which was that of the Middle Ages.

The Muslim expansion in the seventh century placed two hostile civilizations on the Mediterranean, and "the sea which had hitherto been the centre of Christianity became its frontier. The Mediterranean unity was shattered.". . . This was the most essential event of European history that had occurred since the Punic Wars. It was the

From Daniel C. Dennett, Jr., "Pirenne and Muhammad," *Speculum,* XXIII (April, 1948), pp. 165–190. By permission of The Medieval Academy of America, Cambridge, Mass. [Dr. Dennett's extensive documentation, save for a few references for quotations, has been omitted.]

end of the classic tradition. It was the beginning of the Middle Ages." The sea was closed to Gaul about the year 650, since the first raid on Sicily came two years later. As a result, the last text mentioning oils and spices is dated 716 and may be a hasty recopy of a charter of 673–675. There is not a single mention of spices in any document of the Carolingian period. The wines of Gaza and the papyrus of Egypt disappeared, silk was entirely unknown, and North African oil was cut off, with the result that churches turned from lamps to candles. The coinage was debased and gold yielded to silver. The Merovingian merchant, defined as a *negotiator* who "lent money at interest, was buried in a sarcophagus, and gave of his goods to the churches and the poor," ceased to exist.

Inasmuch as Pirenne has based his entire thesis on the influence of commerce, he is compelled to give a somewhat novel explanation of the political disintegration of Merovingian Gaul under the *rois fainéants*. He argues that the commercial decline due to the Arabs began about the year 650, that this epoch corresponds almost exactly with the progress of anarchy in Gaul, that the only source of the king's power was money, money which was derived in largest measure from the indirect taxes (*tonlieu*) on commerce, that the royal power, weakened by loss of revenue, had to compromise with the church and the nobility, that immunities were therefore not the cause of the king's weakness but in reality were a consequence of it, and that thus the progress of Islam destroyed the Merovingians.

Furthermore, the shattering of Mediterranean unity restricted the authority of the Pope to Western Europe, and the conquest of Spain and Africa by the Arabs left the king of the Franks the master of the Christian Occident. This king was the only temporal authority to whom the Pope could turn, and therefore "it is strictly correct to say that without Mohammed, Charlemagne would have been inconceivable."

In summation, "If we consider that in the Carolingian epoch the minting of gold had ceased, that lending money at interest was prohibited, that there was no longer a class of professional merchants, that Oriental products (papyrus, spices, silk) were no longer imported, that the circulation of money was reduced to the minimum, that laymen could no longer read and write, that the taxes were no longer organized, and that the towns were merely fortresses, we can say without hesitation that we are confronted with a civilization which had retrogressed to the purely agricultural stage; which no longer needed commerce, credit, and regular exchange for the maintenance of the social fabric." The Muslim conquest had transformed the economic world from the money economy of the Merovingians to the natural economy of the Middle Ages.

A critic of Pirenne's theses must begin by asking the following six questions:

1. Was it the policy and the practice of the Arabs to prohibit commerce either at its source or on the normal trade routes of the Mediterranean? Can we indicate an approximate date, accurate within twenty-five years, for the ending of commerce between the Christian Occident and the Orient?

2. Is it possible to find another explanation for the disappearance of the wines of Gaza, the papyrus of Egypt, and the spices of the Orient?

3. Is it true that Gaul had no appreciable foreign commerce after the beginning of the Carolingian period?

4. Is it true that the civilization of Merovingian Gaul, considered in its broadest social and political aspects, was determined by trade? Is it possible that internal factors conversely may have been of importance in determining the prosperity of industry and trade? How extensive was Mediterranean commerce before 650?

5. Was "Romania" in fact a true cultural unity of ideas, law, language, foreign policy, common interest?

6. What is the real significance and true cause of the transition from a gold to a silver coinage?

I

We must affirm that neither in the Koran, nor in the sayings of the Prophet, nor in the acts of the first caliphs, nor in the opinions of Muslim jurists is there any prohibition against trading with the Christians or unbelievers. Before Muhammad, the Arabs of the desert lived by their flocks and those of the town by their commerce. To these two sources of livelihood the conquest added the income of empire and the yield of agriculture, but the mercantile career remained the goal of many, as the caravan still crossed the desert and the trading vessel skirted the coast line of the Red Sea, the Persian Gulf, and the Indian Ocean. Pirenne had asserted that "it is a proven fact that the Musulman traders did not instal themselves beyond the frontiers of Islam. If they did trade, they did so among themselves." This statement is a serious misrepresentation of fact. Arab merchants had established trading colonies which were centers not only for the exchange of goods but the propagation of the faith in India, Ceylon, the East Indies, and even China, by the close of the eighth century, and if one wishes to know why they did not establish similar centers in Gaul, let him ask the question — would Charlemagne have permitted a mosque in Marseilles?

In this respect the Muslims themselves were more tolerant and placed few obstacles in the path of Christian traders who came to their territory. Within the lands that had formerly submitted to the Emperor, the Christians were now subjects of the Muslim state, yet they were protected by law, and in return for the payment of their taxes and the discharge of obligations stipulated in the original terms of capitulation, they were specifically and formally guaranteed the freedom of Christian worship, the jurisdiction of Christian bishops in cases not involving Muslims, and the pursuit of trades and professions. The civil service and the language of administration remained Greek, and Arabic did not universally displace Greek in the government bureaus until the end of the first century

following the conquest. In Egypt, at least, the change of rule brought an improvement in the social and economic life of the population, and the church of Alexandria enjoyed a liberty of faith which it had hitherto not experienced.

In consideration of the fact that it has formerly been believed that internal causes produced a decline of industry and trade in Gaul, the burden of proof in Pirenne's thesis must show that the Arab raids were of a frequency and intensity *in themselves* to destroy the commerce of the western Mediterranean. It is not a just argument merely to assert that these raids were disastrous because commerce in Gaul declined. We have already noticed that in order to connect the decline of the Merovingian monarchy with the activity of the Arabs, Pirenne has been obliged to assign the date 650 as that point when Arab naval activity became formidable. What are the facts?

There may have been a raid on Sicily in 652. We are told that it was led by Muawia ibn Hudaij and resulted in taking much booty from unfortified places, but was called off when plague threatened the invaders. As Amari shows, there is a great deal of confusion among the Muslim authorities both as to the date (for an alternative, 664 A.D. is given), as to the leader (since it is highly probable that not Muawia but his lieutenant Abdallah ibn Qais commanded the actual expedition), and as to the port of embarkation (either Tripoli in Syria or Barka in North Africa). Becker does not accept the date 652 and argues that the first raid took place only in 664, but it is possible that there were two different expeditions, one in 652, the second in 664.[1]

Three years after the presumed earliest assault on Sicily, the Emperor Constans II, in 655, received a serious blow to his prestige when the Byzantine fleet was beaten in the Aegean by the new Muslim navy in

[1] Amari is an Italian historian and C. H. Becker was Professor of Oriental History in the Colonial Institute of Hamburg. Dennett's references to their writings have been omitted. [Editor's note]

the first real test of sea power. The Arabs did not follow up their victory, but its consequence demonstrated to the Emperor the need for a vigorous naval policy, for, although Constantinople and the straits might be held against siege, the strategically vulnerable point of the Empire was not in the Aegean, but in the West, since (as events were to show two centuries later) once the enemy had a base in Sicily, South Italy would then be within easy grasp, and if South Italy were securely held, only immense naval exertions could protect Greece proper, and if Greece fell under Muslim control, a combined blockade by land and sea of the imperial city would be possible. Bury[2] holds that this consideration, the guarding of the rear against attack from the West, was a strong motive in inducing Constans to concentrate naval power in the West and to go himself to Sicily in 662, where he reigned for six years until his assassination in 668.

The Arabs took advantage of the chaos following the assassination to raid the coasts of Sicily the next year, but when order was reestablished Sicily remained at peace again for thirty-five years.

Meanwhile the Greek fleet itself was far from inactive, raiding Egypt in 673 and, in a successful attack on Barka in 689, putting the Arabs to rout in which the governor of North Africa, Zuheir ibn Qais, perished. Early attempts to take Carthage were frustrated because the Greeks had control of the seas, and the city fell in 698 only because the Arabs had constructed a fleet for the purpose and the Greek naval force was in the Aegean. Following Bury's argument, if the Emperor had established a permanent naval base at Carthage, the city would never have been taken.

Therefore, in view of the facts that the Arabs made only two, (possibly three) raids on Sicily before 700, that these raids resulted in a vigorous naval policy of the Greeks in the West, that it was not until

698 that the Arabs had a fleet strong enough to operate at Carthage, and that they had not yet seized the straits of Gibraltar or occupied Spain, we are bound to acknowledge the absence of any evidence to indicate the closing of the Mediterranean thereby weakening the basis of royal power in Gaul before 700. Pirenne himself acknowledges this fact by admitting that spices and papyrus could be procured by the monks of Corbie in 716. Indeed, anyone who reads Pirenne closely will notice that he is careless with chronology and mentions results which were produced by the Arab conquest as beginning at various points within a period of 150 years.

What progress was made in the eighth century? In 700 the Arabs took Pantellaria and constructed a naval base in Tunis with the intention of undertaking the conquest of Sicily, but after some preliminary raids in 703–705, for the purpose of reconnoitering, the new governor, Musa ibn Nusair, turned westwards and launched a campaign which was to culminate in the Spanish conquest, begun in 711.

Papyri dated 710 to 718 give us considerable information about ship building in the Nile delta, where vessels were constructed for service not only in Egypt but in the West and in Syria as well, and mention raids of which, unfortunately, we know neither the destination nor the results. We do not know of any raids against Sicily until 720. Thereafter there were attacks in 727, 728, 730, 732, and 734. It must be emphasized that these were not attempts at conquest nor were they successful against fortified ports. A raid in 740 was recalled when civil war, due to tribal and religious factions, broke out throughout the entire territory under Muslim sway, a war which ended all hopes of an Arab offensive and resulted in the destruction of the Umayyad Caliphate at Damascus. In the meantime the Greek fleet led attacks on Egypt in 720 and 739, won a naval victory in 736, and annihilated the principal Arab force off Cyprus in 747. Only three Arab ships escaped this disaster.

[2] J. B. Bury (d. 1927) was a distinguished British historian, an authority on the later Roman Empire and the Byzantine era. [Editor's note]

After 751 the new Arab capital was 700 miles from the sea, and the Abbasids neglected the navy. Spain became independent under a rival Umayyad, and the political control of North Africa weakened sensibly. Henceforth naval operations could be undertaken only by virtually independent governors who lacked the organization and collective resources of the Caliphate. A last abortive assault on Sicily in 752–753 was frustrated by the Greek fleet. A fifty years peace followed, perpetuated in 805 in a treaty signed by Ibrahim ibn Aghlab for a term of ten years and renewed by his son for a similar period in 813. The Arab conquest of Sicily did not commence until 827 and then only on invitation of a rebel Greek who had assassinated the governor.

Sardinia was first raided in 710 and Corsica in 713. The Arab control of the latter ended with its reconquest by Charlemagne in 774, and the Arab occupation of Sardinia was never complete. We have no evidence that these islands were used as bases for raids on commerce.

Pirenne grants that after 717 there was no question of Arab superiority in the Aegean but argues that before that time Arab naval activity had serious consequences. We have already noted that during the seventh century the Greeks for much of the time were sure enough of their Aegean position to conduct raids against Egypt and North Africa and to operate in the West. Let us review briefly the situation.

In 655, an Arab fleet routed the Greeks led by Constans II. This was the first and only *important* naval defeat. The following year the caliph Uthman was murdered, and in the ensuing struggle for power between Ali and Muawia, the latter, to secure his rear and the Syrian coasts against a Greek assault, entered into an arrangement in 659 with the Emperor by which he agreed to pay tribute. In 666, according to Theophanes,[3] the Mardaites, an unconquered

people inhabiting the Amanus mountains in Northwest Syria, broke out in a series of attacks which secured for them all the strategic points from northern Syria to Palestine. It is presumed that Muawia, after being recognized as caliph, had ceased to pay tribute, but this new situation made it impossible to defend the Syrian ports should the Greek fleet determine to attack, and again the caliph, to secure his position, resumed the payment of tribute.

During the years 674–680 men witnessed the first "siege" of Constantinople. The Arab fleet established a winter base at Cyzicus in the Propontis and raided the Aegean in the summer. We have no evidence that their operations severed communications between Constantinople and the West, which could be maintained by land anyway, and trade with the East was still possible via the Black Sea port of Trebizond.

Armenia during the Sassanid rule of Persia was obligatory neutral territory for the exchange of goods between East and West, inasmuch as a national of the one country was prohibited from setting foot on the territory of the other. Trebizond on the Black Sea was the port of entry, and Dwin, among other towns, was a principal mart of the interior. After the Muslim conquest, Armenia, the friend of the Greeks and the vassal of the Arabs, continued to remain a center for the exchange of goods.

In 685, Abdul Malik, faced with a civil war in Iraq, resumed payment of the tribute of Muawia to protect his western flank, and the agreement was renewed for a five year period in 688 with the condition, among others, that the tribute from the island of Cyprus, which had been recovered by the Greeks, should be equally divided between the Greeks and the Arabs. The truce was violated in 691–692 by the Emperor when he declined to accept the new Arab coinage and violated the Cyprus convention. The last great assault on Constantinople was the siege of 716–718. Greek fire terrified the enemy, and the failure of the Arab fleet to provision the besiegers resulted in catastrophe. Only five

[3] Theophanes, 758–817, a Byzantine chronicler. [Editor's note]

Muslim vessels escaped destruction and but a remnant of the army reached Syria.

When we consider that the three attempts on Constantinople all failed, that only during the years 774–780 did a Muslim fleet dominate the Aegean, that the Greeks had recovered Cyprus, and that for long periods the two most powerful caliphs, Muawia and Abdul Malik, paid tribute to the Greeks to preserve the Syrian ports from attack, we are not justified in saying that Arab naval supremacy broke up the Greek lines of communication in the Aegean during the seventh century.

Finally, let us consider the possibility that Gaul was cut off from the East by military occupation.

The Arabs crossed the Pyrenees in 720, occupied Narbonne, and controlled the extreme southern part of the country bordering on the Mediterranean — Septimania. In 726 they occupied Carcassonne. The next great advance, coming in 732, was turned back by Charles Martel in the celebrated battle of Tours. In 736 they reached the Rhone for the *first* time at Arles and Avignon but were hurled back the next year by Charles. We have already mentioned the period of chaos after 740 which shelved all plans of aggression; when domestic order was restored, a new power existed in Gaul; Pippin recaptured Narbonne in 759. Pirenne himself says, "This victory marks, if not the end of the expeditions against Provence, at least the end of the Musulman expansion in the West of Europe." Charlemagne, as is well known, carried the war with indifferent success across the Pyrenees, but the Arabs did not again renew their assaults until after his death. In 848 they raided Marseilles for the first time, and later, spreading out from the base at Fraxinetum, pushed into Switzerland, where in 950 they held Grenoble and the St Bernard Pass. The consequences of this activity, however, fall long after the period under discussion and need not be considered here.

To summarize: It is not correct to assume, as Pirenne does, that a policy of economic blockade played as principal a role in the warfare of antiquity and the Middle Ages as it does today, unless there is a positive testimony to that effect, as for example, the instance when the Persians cut the Greeks off from the supply of Eastern silk. With the exception of two brief intervals, the Byzantine fleet was master of the Aegean and the eastern Mediterranean not only in the seventh century but in the following centuries. This same fleet defended the West so well that only two raids are known to have been attempted against Sicily before 700. After the conquest of Spain had been accomplished, the Arabs embarked in 720 on an ambitious policy which took them for one brief year to the Rhone, and exactly coinciding in time with these military attacks came a series of raids on Sicily; but by 740 dismal failure was the reward everywhere, and throughout the last fifty years of the century the Arabs were either at peace or on the defensive.

We cannot admit that this evidence permits one to say, "Thus, it may be asserted that navigation with the Orient ceased about 650 as regards the regions situated eastward of Sicily, while in the second half of the 7th century it came to an end in the whole of the Western Mediterranean. By the beginning of the 8th century it had completely disappeared."

The synchronization of land and sea attacks, between 720 and 740, was repeated a hundred years later, for, as Sicily was being reduced, the invaders again crossed the Pyrenees. There is little probability that such synchronization was deliberate, but on this second occasion it was terribly effective. Then, if ever, Pirenne's thesis ought to apply; for once the enemy held the southern coast of France and Sicily in full conquest, as well as Southern Italy and the port of Bari, thus constituting a threat to any navigation in the Adriatic, one would imagine that all commerce must have ceased. The remarkable fact is that this is the very period when we begin to have comparatively full records of the commerce between the Arabs on one side, and Naples, Amalfi, Sorrento, Gaeta, and the rising state of Venice on the other side. This commerce prospered despite all efforts of Pope and Emperor to suppress it. Jules Gay, the eminent authority on the history of Southern Italy in this epoch, has truly observed: "In these last years of the ninth century when the Arab domination furnished the conquest of the Island [Sicily], the hegemony of Islam in the Mediterranean already had found its limit in the restoration of Byzantine power in the south of Italy on the shores of the Ionian Sea at the entrance of the Adriatic. But let us not forget that a conquest, quite recent, of the greater part of Sicily had been necessary to establish this hegemony. Sicily, remaining entirely Byzantine until 830, succeeded in maintaining in a large measure its former relations between the two parts of the Mediterranean world. To suppose that the conquest of Syria and of Egypt between 630 and 640 had been responsible for the severing of the ancient Mediterranean unity, the closing of the sea, the isolating of the Orient from the Occident, as Pirenne seems to believe, is to exaggerate singularly the consequence and the extent of the first Arab victories . . . . The final overthrow was not the work of a single generation; it took place more slowly than one would imagine. Carthage remained Byzantine till 698 and a century yet had to pass for the Arab navy to affirm its preponderance in the Western basin of this sea."

II

Did the Arab conquest of Egypt in 640–642 end the exportation of papyrus? The evidence is to the contrary. It was not until 677 that the royal chancery of Gaul adopted parchment and it would be difficult to imagine that the Frankish government had a supply on hand to last for thirty-seven years. Actually, papyrus was employed in Gaul until a much later epoch, since the monks of Corbie obtained fifty rolls in 716, but the last specimen, dated 787, discovered in the country, had been written in Italy.

Papyrus was traditionally employed by the papacy. Still preserved on papyrus are numerous papal documents, together with a letter of Constantin V to Pippin and a breviary of Archbishop Peter VI (927–971) describing the possessions of the Church of Ravenna. That papyrus was the customary material used by the popes seems to be indicated by numerous references, e.g., the glossator of the panegyrist of Berengar comments on the word papyrus "secundum Romanum morem dicit, qui in papiro scribere solent."

In light of the evidence, there can be no other conclusion than that "the conquest of Egypt by the Arabs brought no immediate change. The manufacturing of papyrus continued." Relying on a statement of Ibn Haukal who referred to the cultivation of papyrus in Sicily in 977, some have held that in the tenth and eleventh centuries, the papal chancery obtained its supplies in Sicily and not in Egypt. In this connection it is worth noting that the process of making rag paper was introduced from China into the Eastern Caliphate shortly after 750, and we hear of a paper factory in Bagdad in 794. About this time there was a decline in Egyptian production of papyrus, and political disturbances in the country so interfered with a supply which paper had not yet made dispensable, that the caliph was forced to establish his own papyrus factory at Samarra in 836. T. W. Allen suggests that inasmuch as the earliest known Greek minuscule occurs in the Uspensky Gospels of 835, one may accept as a hypothesis that a known temporary shortage of papyrus may have induced the world of the Isaurian monarchy to give up the use of papyrus, to write on vellum only, in book form, on both sides, in a small hand permitting the most to be made of the space. Papyrus continued to be produced until the competition of paper finally destroyed the industry in the middle of the eleventh century, and the fact that the last Western document to employ it, a bull of Victor II, is dated 1057 and coincides with the end of production in Egypt, leads us to believe that it was on Egypt, and not on Sicily, that the papacy depended.

Parchment, of course, was not unknown in Merovingian Gaul. Gregory of Tours mentions it, as Pirenne points out. It was regularly employed in preference to papyrus in Germany from the earliest times.

Since the Arab conquest of Egypt did not cut off the supply of papyrus at its source, because this material was still found in Gaul a century later and was regularly employed by the papacy until the eleventh century, it is difficult to say that its disappearance in Gaul is a conclusive proof that the Arabs had cut the trade routes. In the absence of all direct evidence one way or another, it would appear that as a possible hypothesis one might conclude that because parchment could be locally produced, because it was preferable as a writing material, and because, owing to a depreciated coinage, it *may* not have been more expensive than papyrus, the people of Gaul preferred to employ it.

The wines of Gaza undoubtedly were no longer exported, or even produced on a large scale, since it is a not unreasonable assumption that the Arabs, following the well known Koranic injunction against wine, discouraged its manufacture. Some vineyards certainly remained, for the Christian churches of Palestine and Syria still used wine in celebrating the mass, and certain of the later Umayyad Caliphs were notorious drunkards. But inasmuch as papyrus and (as we shall presently show) spices were still exported, the *argumentum ad vinum* cannot be seriously advanced.

III

Is it true that with the Carolingians the former commerce of Gaul came to an end and the importation of Eastern luxuries ceased?

Everyone agrees — even Pirenne — that Gaul was surrounded by countries actively engaged in commerce. In Italy, for example, Venetian traders were selling velvet, silk, and Tyrian purple in Pavia by 780. Early in the ninth century they had trad-

ing connections with Alexandria, since the Doge issued an edict in conjunction with Leo V (813–820) forbidding this trade — an edict which had little effect in view of the fact that Venetian merchants translated the body of St Mark in 827. Venice exported armor, timber for shipbuilding, and slaves — the latter despite the interdicts of Charlemagne and Popes Zacharias and Adrian I and imported all the usual Eastern products: spices, papyrus, and silks, large quantities of which were purchased by the Papacy.

Confronted with the alternative of defending Christendom or cooperating with the Saracens in return for trading rights, Naples, Amalfi, Salerno, and Gaeta chose the latter course.

North of Gaul, the Scandinavian countries and the region about the Baltic maintained an active intercourse with Persia via the water routes of Russia. The Arabs purchased furs (sable, ermine, martin, fox, and beaver), honey, wax, birch bark (for medicinal purposes), hazel nuts, fish glue, leather, amber, slaves, cattle, Norwegian falcons, and isinglas (made from sturgeons' bladders), and they sold jewelry, felt, metal mirrors, luxury goods, and even harpoons for the whale fisheries, besides exporting large quantities of silver coin to balance an unfavorable trade. The evidence for the really great prosperity of this commerce is to be found in the enormous coin hoards, the contents of tombs excavated in Scandinavia, the accounts of Arab geographers, and the incidental references in the writings and lives of men like Adam of Bremen and St Ansgar.[4] Pirenne testifies to the importance of commerce in this period for the Netherlands.

We now come to the crucial point. If Gaul was surrounded by neighbors actively engaged in commerce, did not some of their activity embrace Gaul as well? Pirenne de-

[4] Adam of Bremen (11th century) wrote *The Deeds of the Bishops of Hamburg-Bremen,* a valuable source for North German history. St. Ansgar (9th century) was the first Christian missionary to the Swedes; his life was written by Rimbert, a contemporary. [Editor's note]

nies this and asserts that no mention of spices is to be found after 716 in Gaul and that no *negotiator* of the Merovingian type — a man who lent money at interest, was buried in a sarcophagus, and bequeathed property to the poor and the church — existed.

Now spices could be obtained at the time of Charlemagne, but at a high price, according to a statement of Alcuin, "Indica pigmentorum genera magno emenda pretio." Augsburg, from the beginning of the tenth century, imported oriental products via Venice. In 908 we read of a gift of Tyrian purple by the bishop of Augsburg to the monastery of St Gall. . . .

Einhard, in his account of the translation of the blessed martyrs, Marcellinus and Peter, mentions that the holy relics on arrival were placed on *new* cushions of silk and that the shrine was draped with fine linen and silk. Abbo, in his epic of the siege of Paris by the Northmen in 885–886, scorned those whose manners were softened by Eastern luxuries, rich attire, Tyrian purple, gems, and Antioch leather. Similar references are to be found in the work of the celebrated monk of St Gall.[5] Are we certain that this credulous retailer of myth completely falsified the local color as well? A far more interesting example is a long list of spices to be found appended to a manuscript of the statutes of Abbot Adalhard. These statutes are certainly dated in 822, but the manuscript is a copy of 986, so scholars have assumed the possibility that the list of spices may have been inserted at any period between 822 and 986. If this were true, Pirenne's case would certainly be shaken and he has not hesitated to deny the authenticity of the document, which he places in the Merovingian period. But he can produce not a single argument to support his view — except the usual one — the document could not date from 822 or after because the Arabs had cut the trade routes

of the Mediterranean. Such a reason is inadmissible.

That Carolingian Gaul traded with her neighbors we may gather from a capitulation issued by Charlemagne in 805 regulating commerce with the East in which specific towns were named where merchants might go. Louis the Pious confirmed the bishop of Marseilles as collector of tariff at the port. An edict of Charles III in 887 mentions merchants at Passau on the Danube who were exempt from customs duties. A pact of Lothar in 840 regulated trade with Venice.

Charles the Bald in a charter of immunity given to St Denis in 884 exempted from all exactions boats belonging to the monks engaged in trade or to their commercial agents, . . .

Sabbe has discovered an example of at least one *negotiator* who died in Bonn in 845 and disposed of a large estate — a man who certainly would seem to be included in Pirenne's definition of a Merovingian merchant. We have a continuous record of Mainz as a trading center from the ninth to the eleventh century: Einhard mentions grain merchants who were accustomed (*solebant*) to make purchases in Germany. The *Annales Fuldenses*, for the famine year of 850, mention the price of grain there. Frisian merchants founded a colony in the city in 866. Otto I sent a wealthy merchant of Mainz as ambassador to Constantinople in 979. An Arab geographer of the next century describing the city says, "It is strange, too, that one finds there herbs which are produced only in the farthest Orient: pepper, ginger, cloves, etc." Sabbe has collected much evidence, from which he concludes that in the ninth and tenth centuries there were merchants, men of fortune, making long voyages, transporting cargoes in ships they owned personally and speculating on the rise of prices. . . .

Any notion that Gaul was separated from commercial contacts with the East in the ninth and tenth centuries can be contradicted by irrefutable evidence.

[5] These were the *Annals of St. Gaul,* written in the famous monastery in Switzerland.

IV

Is it true that the culture and stability of Merovingian Gaul was largely determined by its commerce? The answer to this question is to be found in a brief survey of the economic history of the country. From the Roman conquest until the end of the second century of our era, Gaul enjoyed an immense prosperity based on natural products. Wheat and barley were produced in exportable quantities. Flax and wool were woven into textiles famous throughout the Mediterranean world. Cicero tells us (*De Republica,* III, 9, 16) that Rome, to safeguard Italian interests from competition, forbade the production of wine and olives, but the prohibition was ineffective as vineyards and olive orchards multiplied. The wine of Vienne was especially prized in Rome and in the middle of the second century Gaul exported both oil and olives. Forests yielded timber which was sawed into planking or exported to feed the fires of the baths of the imperial city. In Belgium horses were bred for the Roman cavalry. Ham, game birds, and the oysters of Medoc were prized by Roman gourmets.

Mines yielded copper, lead, and iron, and quarries in the Pyrenees, marble. Especially famous was Gallic pottery and glass, large quantities of which have been found at Pompeii and in Naples and Rome. The names of hundreds of free workers are known from autographs on sherds. The principal industries were textiles and ironware, for Gallic swords, armor, and metal utensils were highly valued. Leather and skin containers for oil were widely manufactured. One fact is of the *utmost* importance: the merchants and shipowners who carried this commerce were of Gallo-Roman birth. The merchants of Narbonne[6] had a *schola* at Ostia as did those of Arles. An inscription in Narbonne tells us that a native merchant of that city who traded in Sicily was an honorary magistrate of all

the important Sicilian ports. Another inscription found in Beirut, dated 201, contains a letter of the prefect to representatives of the five corporations of *navicularii* of Arles. It should be especially noted that all the commodities mentioned above have one characteristic in common: they are either bulky or heavy objects of low intrinsic value which depend of necessity for profitable export on cheap transportation and relative freedom from onerous tariffs.

The accession of Commodus in 180 marks the beginning of serious civil disturbances in Gaul. Robber bands pillaged the country. After his assassination in 192, the struggle between Clodius and Septimus Severus was settled in the battle of Lyon, in the course of which the city was sacked and burned. Political disorder in this and ensuing periods was always an invitation for the barbarians to cross the frontier. They now came in bands, inflicting damage everywhere. Alexander Severus restored some semblance of order and initiated a policy of settling the new arrivals in military colonies on the frontier, but assassination stayed his hand and the infamous Maximin, who dominated the scene after 235, systematically confiscated all property within his grasp. He reduced the most illustrious families to poverty, seized the property of the different societies and charitable foundations, and stripped the temples of their valuables. A treasure hoard uncovered in 1909 in Cologne, of 100 gold aurei and 20,000 silver pieces, dating from Nero to 236, testifies to the unhappy fate of the owner, who preserved his goods but doubtless lost his life. Maximin shortly was slain, but civil war continued from 238 to 261, with new invasions of Franks and Alemans in 253–257. In 267 the German soldiery murdered the emperor, who had forbidden them the sacking of Mainz. When Aurelian died in 275 more barbarians entered Gaul, to be checked until Probus died in 282, when Alemans and Burgundians ravaged the country and pirates harried the coasts. At the same time the terrible Bagaudes,

[6] Narbonne, in southern France, in the Middle Ages had a port on the Mediterranean. [Editor's note]

robber bands of peasants, wreaked havoc wherever they went. It is highly significant that in the debris scattered about Roman ruins in France today are to be found coins and scattered inscriptions dating about, but rarely after, the second half of the third century, thus fixing the date of the greatest damage. Adrian Blanchet, in a study of 871 coin hoards uncovered in Gaul and northern Italy, by tabulating the results in chronological and geographical form has concluded that there is a remarkable correspondence between the places and periods of disorder and invasion, and the location, numbers, and size of the hoards.

When order was restored in the fourth century, the cities had been reduced to a size which could be easily fortified and defended, and they became important rather as military centers with a population of officials, soldiers, clerics, and a few merchants, than as the once thriving, proud, free cities of happier eras. An attempt was made at reconstruction, as in the case of Autun, ravaged in 269 and restored in the years after 296. Testifying to the lack of skilled labor was the importation of masons from Britain to assist in the rebuilding. Yet when Constantine visited Autun in 311 it was still poor and sparsely settled, while the citizens who survived complained of the crushing taxation.

Renewed civil war followed the death of Constantine in 337, culminating in the Frankish invasion of 355. Julian's campaigns brought peace and a revitalized life, but the year following his death, 363, the Alemans again invaded the country and in 368 sacked Mainz. After 395 Gaul was virtually abandoned by the Empire.

In addition to these civil disturbances, the depreciation of the Roman coinage in the third century was a powerful factor in leading to the institution of the colonnate and compulsory services of the fourth century with attendant hardships on the poor and middle classes. The severity of their circumstances urged them to seek relief through the relationship of the *precarium* and *patrocinium,* producing as the result

the dominating class of the great landholders of the senatorial aristocracy and a general weakening of all imperial authority.

One would imagine that the final product of these disturbances and regulations would be the serious, if not catastrophic deterioration of the once flourishing economic activity of the country, and our information leads us to believe that such was the case. Some cloth was still made at Treves, Metz, and Reims; but, if we except the beautiful jewelry of the Merovingian age, the glass industry alone may be said to have flourished, although the pieces that have survived are poor in quality and design and characterized by imperfect purification of the glass. Technical skill in masonry was limited, and the crudity of lettering on inscriptions bears witness to a decline of craftsmanship. During the earlier period of the empire, there were frequent references to Gallic sailors, as we have shown, but in the fourth century we hear only of African, Spanish, Syrian, and Egyptian sailors, and it is, of course, well known that Syrians and Orientals henceforth play an increasingly dominant role in trade and commerce. It would be a serious mistake to exaggerate this decline. Arles was still a busy port for the entrance of Eastern commodities, as an edict of Honorius of 418 testifies, and some possessors of large estates were extremely wealthy not only in land, but in large sums of gold; however, the accumulative testimony of writers, archaeology, and legislation indicates a far smaller scale of activity in industry and commerce then two centuries earlier.

Consequently, if after the Gothic invasions of North Italy, Southern Gaul, and Spain, and the Vandal conquest of North Africa and pirate raids in the western Mediterranean in the fifth century, we wish to speak of commerce as a determining factor in Merovingian Gaul, we would have to show that the reigns of Clovis and his successors produced a considerable economic revival, rather than that they maintained purely the status quo. This is, of course, one of the major parts of Pirenne's thesis:

that there was an important identity in all the significant aspects of life, government, and culture between East and West, a true unity which effected a real survival – indeed revival – of prosperity until the Muslim conquest. Consequently, a comparison of West and East is necessary, and if possible an attempt should be made to show whether Merovingian government acted to encourage or discourage commerce.

v

The government of Merovingian Gaul was a monarchy, absolute in all respects, and if one may judge from the conduct of its rulers as revealed in the history of Gregory of Tours, the monarch had a very imperfect grasp of the "antique" notion of the state as an instrument designed to promote the common welfare. True, Clovis and his successors preserved many of the features of the Roman administrative system – particularly the method of deriving revenue, but there was certainly not the slightest reason for altering the machinery of an institution designed to raise the maximum of taxes when the principal aim of the ruler was to acquire as much wealth as possible. But even the operation of this part of the government became increasingly inefficient, particularly in the collection of the taxes on land, for the registers were in the greatest disorder and rarely revised, and the powerful did not pay at all. Thus, it came about that the easiest imposts to collect were the indirect tolls on commerce, for officers could be stationed on bridges, at cross roads, in the ports, and along the principal waterways to waylay all who passed. All the old levies of the later empire remained or were multiplied, . . . The internal free trade of a bygone era was a thing of the past, and it should be obvious that while such tariffs could be borne by goods of high intrinsic value and small bulk, or by goods going short distances, they would certainly put an intolerable burden on those products which once constituted the basis of Gaul's prosperity.

True, Latin was still the language of administration, but after the death of Justinian, Greek replaced Latin in the East.

Let us compare the position of King and Emperor. The sovereign of the East was the chief of a hierarchy of subordinate magistrates. He was not above the law, but held himself bound to conform to the accumulated tradition of Roman law and to his own edicts. As ruler, his main preoccupation was the preservation of his empire and its administrative machinery from attacks without and within the state, but he did not hesitate to introduce innovations when circumstances warranted a change. He maintained a standing army and fleet commanded by professional officers whose sworn duty it was to keep the empire secure from all threats. To accomplish all these ends the empire was organized into an administrative bureaucracy, carefully regulated, of extraordinary complexity and detail.

The King of Gaul, on the contrary, thought of himself rather less as a magistrate and rather more as a proprietor. The imperial office in the East was in theory elective, but the King in the West divided his kingdom after his death by rules of inheritance among his several sons without, as Lot has observed, any regard for geography, ethnography, or the desires of the people. Before 476 the unity of East and West, despite the presence of two emperors, was not only theory but fact, for both emperors issued laws under their joint names, and a general law promulgated by one emperor and transmitted to the other for publication was universally valid, but the division of Gaul among the King's sons shattered all legislative unity within the separate kingdoms, and such unity was restored only when and if a more powerful son succeeded in overwhelming and murdering his brothers. Furthermore, an edict issued in Constantinople was neither valid nor binding in Merovingian Gaul – indeed, was probably never heard of. In Gaul the army cost little or nothing, for it was neither professional nor standing, but was recruited by compulsion and without pay when the occasion or emergency warranted. Because a third of the proceeds of judgment went to the King, the courts were regarded more as a source of profit than as instruments of justice. In contrast to the complex bureaucracy of the East, in Gaul the King confided local administration to a few officials who combined executive, financial, and judicial functions in their one person, who commonly purchased their office, and who commonly exercised it to their own profit and the destruction and despair of the inhabitants submitted to their authority.

Pirenne is greatly impressed by the fact that the barbarian states had three features in common with the Empire: they were absolutist, they were secular, and the instruments of government were the fisc and the treasury. This seems to be a similarity without significance or value. Most states ruled by one man are absolutist, secular, and dependent on the treasury — yet that does not prove a derived and intentional identity with Byzantium. The personal role of Charles I before the summoning of the Long Parliament was absolutist; like the Byzantine Emperor, Charles was the head of the church, and his power was exclusively dependent on the treasury, but surely no one would dream of maintaining that there was a valid identity between Stuart England and the Eastern Roman Empire. What earthly reason would Clovis and his successors have had for setting up any other kind of state?

But, still more important, is this supposed identity, even if insignificant, really true? We have already indicated that the absolutism of the Emperor was different in some respects from that of the King. Were both governments *secular* in the same sense and spirit? Pirenne defines a secular government as one conducted without the aid or intervention of the church and its officials, and one in which the King was a pure layman whose power did not depend upon any religious ceremony, although the King might nominate bishops and other clergy and even summon synods.

It is, of course, true that the Byzantine Emperor was a layman in the sense that his power did not depend upon any religious ceremony. Ever since Leo I was crowned in 457 by the Patriarch, that ecclesiastic usually performed the act of coronation, yet, he did so as an important individual — not as a representative of the church — so that his presence was not legally indispensable.

The church, however, was most certainly subject to the state, in a manner utterly unlike that in Gaul, and the union of church and state which became always closer as time went on profoundly affected the character of both. It will be recalled that Constantine had established the principle that it was the emperor's duty and right to summon and preside over general councils of the church, and the later emperors considered themselves competent even to legislate in all religious questions. Justinian, who was a complete Erastian, did so. He issued edicts regulating the election of bishops, the ordination of priests, the appointment of abbots, and the management of church property, nor did he hesitate to pronounce and define his own views, on matters of faith. . . .

If the Emperor, then, played a major role in church affairs, it is also true that the bishops assumed an increasing importance in the civil administration of cities, and Justinian added to their civil functions. They had the right of acting as judges in civil suits when both parties agreed to submit to their arbitration, and judgment once given was not subject to appeal. In municipalities they had the duty of protecting the poor against the tyranny either of the agents of the Emperor or the nobles, and they could appeal directly over the heads of the administrative hierarchy to the Emperor himself. Throughout the territory of the exarchate of Ravenna, the bishops were general supervisors of the baths, granaries, aqueducts, and municipal finance. They protected the poor, prisoners, and slaves. They nominated to the Emperor the candidates for provincial magistracies and assisted at the installation of new governors.

They examined for traces of illegality the acts of civil officials. They received notice before publication of all new laws. In short, they had the recognized power of continual intervention in all matters of secular policy.

Whereas the King of the Franks interfered in the appointment of church officers, he did not pretend to settle larger matters which were reserved for the authority of the Pope, and whereas the Pope's competence was acknowledged in the West, and his claim to be the chief of all bishops was admitted in the East, we have already seen that his authority was frequently challenged and defied by the Emperor, so that a closer examination reveals that far from the Pope and Emperor being mutually indispensable, as Pirenne asserts, the Pope recognized the Emperor's intervention and definition of doctrine only when the temporal authority of the Exarchs was sufficient to compel obedience, or an alliance and cooperation with the Emperor were essential for an immediate papal aim, so that as a general thing it would be more correct to say that from the time of Gregory the Great, the Popes submitted when they must, but asserted their independence when they could. Thus, by Pirenne's own definition of *secular*, it will be seen that there was a very great difference between the state of the Franks and that of the Emperor.

No problem is more important than this: why did the Romans preserve the Empire in the East and lose it to the barbarians in the West? Various answers have been given: the impregnable situation of Constantinople and the more strongly fortified towns of the East, the more favorable geographical factors, the occupation of the throne by men of real ability in times of crisis, and the purely fortuitous turn of events at many times. Of the many factors one should not underestimate two: the character of the emperors and of the citizen population in the East. Both ruler and ruled composed a society which through the traditions of centuries had become accustomed to the idea of the State as an instrument for the very preservation and well-being of society, and to this concept of living under law administered by the officials of government both ruler and ruled paid homage and acknowledged the obligation. Thus there was a community of thought for self-preservation. Unfortunately in the West the same sentiments had not been a sufficient bulwark to keep out the invaders, and the newcomers to power, however much of the paraphernalia of the previous government they may have taken over, certainly failed to absorb, or absorbed but imperfectly, the old notions of the nature of the state and the value of its traditions. The principal fact of the Merovingian period was the decomposition of public power. The refinements of statecraft were an unappreciated art to the wielders of a purely personal power, and this blindness to realities led the kings to take those measures which resulted in the sapping of their own authority. The granting of immunities has long been recognized as a short-sighted act, productive of decay of royal absolutions. Inasmuch as we have already demonstrated that the Arabs did not cut off the trade routes at a time when the effects of their acts could have resulted in the granting of immunities due to weakening of power by the loss of revenue, Pirenne's interpretation of the proper sequence of cause and effect may be rejected. Indeed, we first learn of the granting of immunities in the sixth century, and after 623 the instances become increasingly numerous; the practice was well established long before anyone knew who Muhammad was, and Fustel de Coulanges has well remarked, "Immunity does not date from the decadence of the Merovingian; it is almost as ancient as the Frankish monarchy itself."[7]

In a wild and bloody period where one Merovingian fought another, the reckless expenditure of money, the destruction of property, the escape of the nobility from taxation, the conciliation of partisans by

[7] Fustel de Coulanges, *Les Origines du Systeme Féodal* (Paris, 1907), 345. [Dennett's note]

lavish gifts, — these, and similar factors weakened the royal authority.

Pirenne asserts that "the foreign policy of the Empire embraced all peoples of Europe, and completely dominated the policy of the Germanic State." The fact that on certain occasions embassies were sent to Constantinople or that the Emperor at one time hired the Franks to attack the Lombards is the chief basis of this assertion. Clovis may have been honored by the title of "consul," but would anyone maintain that he considered himself answerable to the will of the Emperor? Insofar as for much of the time the conduct of the kings either in their domestic or foreign affairs can hardly be honored by the term "policy," it would be probably true to say that the Emperor was the *only* one to have a foreign policy.

Again, Pirenne makes a great point of the fact that the Merovingians for a long time employed the image of the Emperor on their coins. So did the Arabs, until Abdul Malik's reform, and for the same reason.

In fact, in matters of law, of policy domestic and foreign, of language, of culture, of statecraft and political vision, the kingdom of the Franks and the empire of the Greeks were as independent of one another as two different sovereign states can be, and if one is reduced to speaking of the mystical "unity of Romania" as a dominant historical fact, one has reduced history itself to mysticism.

Now to return again, after this digression, to the problem of commerce in Merovingian Gaul. It must be clear that there is nothing which one can indicate as calculated to improve the economic prosperity of the country. Furthermore, three characteristics dominate the picture:

1. People of Oriental origin appear to play the chief role in commerce.

2. These Syrians are dealing in luxury goods of eastern origin: spices, papyrus, wines.

3. We have practically no mention at all of exports from Gaul to the East.

Is there any connection between these three facts and the internal political and social condition of the country?

First: There is a physical factor in transportation too often ignored. Goods of high value and small compass may be transported long distances, in face of hardship and peril, and still be sold for a profit. This circumstance alone accounts for the survival and prosperity of the land route of five thousand miles across Central Asia, since tightly baled silk carried by camel and other pack animals was valuable enough to offset the cost of transportation. For the same reason, spices which had already passed through the hands of at least three or four middlemen before reaching a Mediterranean port could be taken to Gaul, either by sea or by land, and yield a satisfactory return to those who made the effort. What was true of spices was also true of papyrus and of silk from Byzantium. A merchant with capital enough to purchase a few hundred pounds of pepper, or of cinnamon, or of silk — even though he had to make wide detours, cover difficult terrain, take considerable risks, and pay innumerable tolls — might still expect to make a profit.

But we have already had occasion to point out that during the flourishing years of the late Republic and early Empire, the commercial prosperity of Gaul was founded principally upon the export of the natural products of the country: food stuffs, cheaper textiles, timber, pottery, glass, skin bags, and so forth. These commodities could either be produced in the other parts of the empire, or could be dispensed with altogether. To compete favorably in the imperial marts their export depended on secure and relatively cheap transportation and the absence of oppressive tolls and restrictive legislation. Therefore, when we consider the destruction wrought by the barbarian invasions, the civil turmoil, the depreciation of the coinage, and the impoverishment of the empire in the third century, we should expect the foreign markets for Gallic products would be temporarily lost, and it would appear reasonable to conclude that the rigid economic and social legislation of the emperors after Diocletian's restoration, the collection of taxes in kind, the multiplication of indirect tolls and tariffs, compulsory services, the fiscal policy of the Frankish kings, and the absence of any policy to promote commerce and economic enterprise, would have made it virtually impossible, even if the desire had existed, to recover and reestablish lost or disorganized markets.

These assumptions have, in fact, commonly been held by most economic historians of the period, and no one has ever produced sufficient evidence seriously to threaten their validity. They are, of course, very inconvenient for Pirenne's thesis. He consequently challenges them, but unfortunately has been unable to find more than one direct piece of evidence: that Gregory the Great purchased some woollen cloth in Marseilles and had some timber sent to Alexandria. He also is "rather inclined" to believe that the Germanic invasions revived the prosperity of the slave trade.

VI

Since this evidence is scarcely convincing, and since it would be difficult to find more, Pirenne turns to the problem of money and says, "In any case, the abundant circulation of gold compels us to conclude that there was a very considerable export trade." Now, in the absence of any banking system for settling by the shipment of bullion an accumulated disparity between exports and imports, one would certainly be prepared to believe it quite possible that the export of some products would bring foreign gold into the country, although the total supply might be diminishing due to larger imports, and this was undoubtedly the case, but Pirenne goes much farther and makes it very plain that he believes the exports from Gaul in early Merovingian days exceeded in value, or at least equalled, the imports of eastern products, since "if it [gold] had been gradually drained away by foreign trade we should find that it diminished as time went on.

But we do not find anything of the sort." He argues that when the Muslim conquest closed the trade routes, gold became a rarity and was abandoned for silver as a medium of exchange. The employment of silver was the real beginning of the Middle Ages and is a witness of a reversion to natural economy. When gold reappeared, the Middle Ages were over, and "Gold resumed its place in the monetary system only when spices resumed theirs in the normal diet."

A natural question arises. If gold remained the medium of currency, unimpaired in quantity due to a favorable export balance until the Arabs cut the trade routes, what happened to it then? It could not have flowed East after the catastrophe on the assumption that exports suffered before imports, because Pirenne is insistent, and all the evidence he has collected is designed to show that it was the import of Eastern products which first disappeared. If gold *could not* flow East, why did it not remain in Gaul as a medium of local exchange?

There are at least three factors in the problem.

1. From the earliest times small quantities of gold were found in the beds of certain streams flowing from the Pyrenees, and even in the sands of the Rhine, but the supply was so negligible that one may assert that the West produced no gold. On the other hand, there were substantial deposits of silver, and there were silver mines at Melle in Poitou and in the Harz mountains.

2. It should be unnecessary to point out that we have not the slightest idea of the total amount of gold in Gaul at any period. We occasionally hear of an amount confiscated by a king, of a loan given by a bishop, of a sum bequeathed the church by a landholder or merchant, of the size of booty or tribute, of a subsidy of 50,000 *solidi* sent by the Emperor, but that is all. In many cases, without doubt, a figure or instance is mentioned, not because it was usual, but because it was extraordinary. The number and importance of coin finds are not in any proportion to the probable facts and may not be relied on. Therefore

when Pirenne speaks of "large" amounts of gold, he is merely guessing. Furthermore, as is well known, there was in general circulation a bronze and silver currency for use in smaller transactions.

3. Gregory the Great (590–604) testifies that Gallic gold coins were so bad that they did not circulate in Italy, and an examination of coins shows a progressive debasement before the Arab conquest. Since these coins did not come from the royal mint, but were struck by roving minters for people in more than a hundred known localities, one has evidence of the chaotic decentralization of the government and lack of interest in orderly financial administration, together with a possible indication of a growing scarcity of gold.

If gold disappeared in Gaul, this disappearance could be due to the following causes:

a. It might have been hoarded, buried, and lost.

b. It might have been exchanged or used for the purchase of silver.

c. It might have been drained off in purchase of commodities in a one sided trade, or paid in tribute.

d. Through the operation of Gresham's law, foreign merchants might have hoarded and removed the good gold coinage, leaving a debased coinage in local circulation.

There is no evidence to support the first two hypotheses, and considerable evidence for the last two — both of which amount to this same fact: gold was drained out of the country. This hypothesis is strongly supported by the best known authority and Bloch gives good reasons for accepting it. Gold, of course, did not completely disappear in the West, as the manufacture of jewelry and occasional references show, and it would be interesting to possess the full facts about the gold coin counterfeiting the Arab dinar — the *mancus*. However, it is difficult to accept the thesis advanced by Dopsch that there was enough gold to constitute with silver a truly bimetallic currency. But it is even more difficult to accept the proposition of Pirenne that the change from gold to silver meant a change from money to natural economy. The numerous instances which prove conclusively that money continued as a medium of exchange have been diligently collected by Dopsch and need not be repeated. It is not clear why silver coinage should equal natural economy. China and Mexico use silver today, and the coins of Arab mintage found in the Baltic regions are also silver, yet no one would pretend that in these instances we are dealing with a system of natural economy. Had a system of natural economy prevailed we might have expected an absence of all kinds of money, and the fact that the Carolingians introduced a pure, standard, centrally minted silver coinage would seem logically to prove just the contrary of Pirenne's thesis. But Pirenne takes as a point the circumstance of the monasteries in those regions of Belgium where the soil will not support vineyards. "The fact that nearly all the monasteries in this region where the cultivation of the vine is impossible, made a point of obtaining estates in the vine-growing countries, either in the valleys of the Rhine and Moselle or in that of the Seine, as gifts from their benefactors, proves that they were unable to obtain wine by ordinary commercial means."[8] Pirenne has drawn his information from an article of Hans van Werveke.[9] The latter appears to have been a collaborator of Pirenne's and asserts, "The phenomenon which we signal is so general that we can say that it responds to an economic law." Now a superficial observer, intent on discovering for himself the likeliest place to observe the functioning of a system of natural self-sufficing economy, might very reasonably turn to a monastery as the logical place of all places, because of monastic rules themselves, to find

---

[8] Pirenne, "The Place of the Netherlands in the Economic History of Medieval Europe," *Economic History Review,* II (1929), 23. [Dennett's note]

[9] Hans van Werveke, "Comment les établissements religieux belges se procuraient-ils du vin au haut moyen âge," *Revue Belge de Philologie et d'Histoire,* II (1923), 643–662. [Dennett's note]

such a system in operation. On the contrary, it is a well known fact that in the Middle Ages a good many monasteries were something more than self-sufficing and turned to advantage surplus commodities which they disposed of, or profited as toll collectors, if rivers, bridge, or roads were within their property. . . .

To conclude: There is no evidence to prove that the Arabs either desired to close, or actually did close the Mediterranean to the commerce of the West either in the seventh or eighth centuries. Islam was hostile to Christianity as a rival, not as a completely alien faith, and the Muslims were invariably more tolerant than the Christians, but Islam as a culture, as the common faith of those who submitted and who spoke Arabic, though not necessarily by any means of Arab blood, had far more in common with the Hellenized East and with Byzantium than did the Gaul of Pirenne's Romania. Much of what he says of Gaul was true of Islam. The Merovingians took over the administrative and particularly the taxation system of Rome intact. So did the Arabs. The Merovingians preserved Latin as the language of administration. The Arabs used Greek. Western art was influenced by Byzantine forms. So was Arab. But these are smaller matters. The crude Western barbarians were not able to develop — indeed, they were too ignorant to

preserve the state and the culture they took by conquest, while the Arabs on the contrary not only preserved what they took but created from it a culture which the world had not known for centuries, and which was not to be equalled for centuries more. This culture was based on that of the Hellenized Eastern Mediterranean in one part and on that of Persia strongly permeated with both Hellenic and Indian elements, on the other. Arab theology, Arab philosophy, Arab science, Arab art — none was in opposition to late antique culture, as Pirenne seems to imagine, but was a new, fertile, virile, and logical development of long established forms. The decadence of the West — the so-called Middle Ages — was due to a complexity of causes, mostly internal, and largely connected with social and political institutions. Rostovtzeff, writing of economic conditions of the later Roman Empire, frequently warns against mistaking an aspect for a cause, and most of the economic factors of the Middle Ages are aspects and not causes. Thus, the man — whether he be a Pirenne or a Dopsch — who attempts to understand and to interpret either the Merovingian or Carolingian period in terms *purely* of an economic interpretation of history will be certain to fail, for the simple reason that economic factors play a subsidiary role and present merely aspects in the great causative process.

THE FATE OF HENRI PIRENNE'S THESES ON THE CONSEQUENCE OF THE ISLAMIC EXPANSION

ANNE RIISING

Anne Riising's article in a Danish journal is a generally successful attempt to summarize the controversy which has developed over the years. She states briefly the essentials of the Pirenne Thesis and then proceeds to an analysis of the evidence and a summary of the views of various historians with respect to that evidence. It is a very comprehensive treatment. The extracts below provide her own statement of the problem and her own conclusions concerning the status of the controversy at the time she writes. There are some slight changes in the order of her material to bring together on particular points her summary questions and her summary conclusions. The student is warned that her essential purpose is merely to bring together the results of research over the years. He should not necessarily adopt her conclusions and should note carefully her own statement, "the last word has certainly not yet been said," and especially her appeal for clearer definitions and for an entire revision of the formulation of the problem itself.

EVERY MEDIEVALIST is acquainted with Henri Pirenne's theses on the consequences of the Islamic expansion, put forward in the years 1922–35. According to these the Roman empire was neither destroyed nor germanized by the Germanic invasions, and "Romania" remained a cultural and economic unity. The best proof of this is to be found in the flourishing commerce of Gaul, to which Syrian merchants, resident in the Occident, imported Oriental spices, wines of Ghaza, oil, papyrus, and luxury cloths. This commerce brought vast quantities of gold to the country, and this money was the foundation of political life, in as much as the king's power was derived from the income obtained by taxes on commerce. The secular classical civilization likewise remained unchanged. But the Islamic expansion crushed the Mediterranean unity and heralded the middle ages. From the middle of the 7th century two hostile civilizations faced each other across the Mediterranean, the sea was closed, and at the beginning of the 8th century all Oriental commerce had come to an end. The urban life and the professional merchants disappeared, gold yielded to silver, money to natural economy, and the king's power collapsed. The Carolingians took the consequences, founded their power on the land, and moved the economic, cultural, and political centre towards the north. The Carolingian kingdom was a purely conti-

From Anne Riising, "The Fate of Henri Pirenne's Theses on the Consequence of the Islamic Expansion," *Classica et Mediaevalia*, XIII (1952), 87–130. Published by Librairie Gyldendal, Copenhagen, 1952, and used with their permission.

nental state, dominated by the Germanic population, whose influence was strengthened by the active mission among heathen Germanic peoples. The character of civilization changed from secular to clerical, education became an ecclesiastical monopoly, and the easy quick cursive was replaced by the calligraphic minuscule. Furthermore, the Islamic expansion restricted the authority of the pope to Western Europe, and since Byzantium could no longer defend Rome against the Lombards, the pope called in the Franks. Thus it is correct to say that without Mohammed, Charlemagne would have been inconceivable.

The thesis is divided into two distinct parts, one showing the continuation of the classical tradition in the Merovingian age, the other demonstrating the fundamental change of society in the Carolingian age. It is, in fact, a new catastrophe theory, giving a novel explanation of the beginning of the middle ages and the making of European civilization. But as the entire thesis is based on the influence of commerce, the literary discussion has mainly concentrated on the problem of the Oriental commerce, and only a few important works have appeared on the cultural development.

ECONOMIC DEVELOPMENT

To judge the importance of the Oriental commerce and its fate after the Islamic expansion three essential problems must be solved:

I. Is it true that Merovingian Gaul had an Oriental commerce of such dimensions as to be the foundation of society and civilization?

II. How and when could the Arabs break off Mediterranean trade, and why did they want to do so?

III. Had the Carolingian age no foreign commerce at all and in particular no Oriental commerce?

I

Is it true that Merovingian Gaul had an Oriental commerce of such dimensions as to be the foundation of society and civilization? . . .

To sum up. An extensive Oriental commerce and a general internal prosperity in the Merovingian age has not been proved and hardly rendered probable. The economic and political development since the 3rd century, combined with the decline of population, suggest a progressive decadence, so that the burden of proof must rest on those who think otherwise. Since nobody has shouldered this burden yet, it is reasonable to assume that the commerce with the Orient was far too small to be the determining factor in Gallic society, and this means that a great part of Pirenne's thesis has collapsed. . . .

II

How and when could the Arabs break off Mediterranean trade, and why did they want to do so?

The first question to be asked is: Had the Arabs power to cut off the commerce at all? They might do so by stopping export from the Moslem countries and blockading the Mediterranean sea routes; or they might shut out Western Europe by military occupation of the Mediterranean coasts; or, finally, the Saracen piracy, though hardly an intended phenomenon, might paralyze navigation. But in no possible way could they cut off land intercourse between Byzantium and Western Europe.

These different possibilities give different answers to the next question, the fixing of the date when the Mediterranean commerce could cease. If the Caliphate immediately embarked on an economic policy with this end in view, it might perhaps have been partly accomplished by the end of the 7th century, provided sufficient naval strength was created. A military occupation could not be effective until the 8th century, and the piracy was of no real importance until the 9th century. But apart from these aspects we must ask one fundamental question: Is it reasonable to assume that the Arabs did intend to cut off Mediterranean commerce, and, if so, what was the reason? If the answer is in the negative, it must finally be investigated, if the making of the Caliphate perhaps brought about such profound changes of international economic conditions that these by themselves led to the end of the commerce between the Orient and the Occident. . . .

To sum up. There is no reason to suppose that the Arabs intended to destroy the Mediterranean commerce, or that they did so either by blockade, military occupation, or piracy. But this does not prove an extensive commerce in the Carolingian kingdom. Considering the earlier development, it was to be expected that the commerce between the Orient and Western Europe, steadily decreasing because of the passive balance of trade, would die a natural death in the Carolingian age. A closer scrutiny of this is necessary.

III

Had the Carolingian age no foreign commerce at all and in particular no Oriental commerce?

It is hardly probable that political or religious contrasts may have caused the Christian Occident to refuse economic relations with the Moslems. Nor could the ecclesiastical disapproval of luxury and scant appreciation of commerce as a whole seriously impede the commercial activity, and though some Oriental products might be replaced by European ones, e.g. papyrus by parchment and oil by fat and butter, the demand for spices and luxury cloths never ceased.

But to judge the extent of the commerce between the Orient and the Christian Occident a number of questions must be answered: Is it true that the Carolingian age did not know Oriental products? Did the Syrian merchants disappear without being replaced by others? Were sea and land routes to the Orient cut off? Was the Carolingian kingdom on the whole characterized by a closed economy without money, especially without gold or other means of paying an import from the Orient? . . .

To sum up. Since the later Roman empire the Occident was in a state of progressive economic decadence, and its Oriental commerce decreased steadily, because the passive balance of trade drained the gold reserves. The Islamic expansion did not bring ruin, for the Arabs neither wanted to nor could destroy the commerce. On the contrary, the immense prosperity within the Caliphate created a demand for Occidental commodities, and by a surplus of exports Western Europe acquired Arabian gold and silver. This enabled the Occident to resume the import from Byzantium, which incidentally contributed to the economic revival of this empire.

But the shape of the international commerce of the Carolingian age was certainly very different from that of the Merovingian age. France itself had hardly any direct communication with the Levant, but traded through Moslem Spain and Byzantine Italy and had an indirect contact via the Baltic and Russia and through Central Europe. The whole of Europe had been involved in the international commerce, which for the first time in history had taken shape of a true interchange. However, the real centre of the Oriental commerce in the Occident was no doubt Italy, while France was of secondary importance, but that was only natural. After all, the Carolingian kingdom was mainly a continental state, and the internal trade and even more the Northern Frisian commerce were no doubt of far greater importance than the Oriental commerce. Though this may have been more extensive than in the Merovingian age, its relative importance was certainly much smaller, and it must not be forgotten that both internal and foreign commerce were far less important than agriculture. Italy, on the other hand, was naturally turned towards the Mediterranean, and the Byzantine provinces were particularly suited to deal in Byzantine commodities. The Italian commerce with Oriental countries was probably of larger dimensions and certainly of far greater relative importance than the French, and it was natural that the Italians, rather than anyone else, should seize on the Oriental commerce.

CULTURAL DEVELOPMENT

Many historians have ventured to judge what may have been the influence of the Islamic expansion on the cultural development of Western Europe, but most of them confine themselves to some general considerations, and very few primary studies have appeared. The entire discussion turns on two central questions:

i. Was the Mediterranean sphere a true cultural unity until the beginning of the 7th century, and was this unity destroyed by Islam?

ii. Was the civilization of the Carolingian age fundamentally different from that of the Merovingian age? . . .

To sum up. In fact very little light has been shed on the immediate effect of the Islamic expansion on the cultural development of Western Europe, and it is unfortunately unlikely that certain results will ever be established, since after all it remains a matter of subjective judgment whether one will speak of a cultural unity or not. From the later Roman Empire a growing difference between the Eastern and the Western Mediterranean indubitably existed, but at the same time they had still much in common compared to that which was outside the orbis romanus. But the Islamic expansion caused no rupture; certainly nobody can deny that from the long view it limited European civilization to Europe proper, but the islamization was a slow process. The Arabs were a small minority in proportion to the conquered peoples; in the Eastern countries they assumed the Hellenistic-Oriental civilization, and in the Western they entered into the Latin heritage, though this proved of much smaller importance.

Nor did Islam break the evolution of Western Europe, and a continuity between the Merovingian and the Carolingian age can hardly be refuted. But evidently the Carolingian age witnessed the outbreak of the east-western antagonism, expressed by the detachment of the papacy and the reconstruction of the western empire. But if the rupture did come in the 8th century,

the reason was probably that the weakening of the Greek empire and the reorganization of the Frankish kingdom had created the necessary actual basis for the new papal policy. Furthermore, the Carolingian conquests included new regions that had had no part in the classical civilization, and, what is more important, the Irish-Anglo Saxon civilization, based on a distinctly Latin tradition, came to dominate the cultural life; this counteracted the Oriental influence and deepened the contrast to the Eastern countries, which in the same period were acquiring a still more markedly Oriental character. The Oriental influence in Italy was certainly strengthened by the immigrations, but the immigrants sided with the papal policy, and that is even truer of the iconodulic refugees in the 8th century.

Thus the most essential influence of the Islamic expansion on the cultural development of the Occident is probably to be found in the fact that the weakening of Byzantium forced this empire to withdraw and leave the Occident peace to pursue its own independent development.

SUMMARY

Research until now had definitely tended towards refuting Pirenne's theses, but the last word has certainly not yet been said. It is, of course, the lack of sources that has made possible so many different views, and though it is preferable to let the sources speak for themselves, they cannot do so. One may quote authorities in support of any theory, and the final judgment of the economic development must consequently depend on a general estimation of the effect which the joint historical course of events may be assumed to have had on the economic conditions. Regarding the consequences of the Islamic expansion specially, the judgment of this problem must, in the end, rest on more or less vague speculations on what would have happened if the Caliphate had not come into existence.

But of course primary examinations of a great many subjects are still needed. Written and archaeological sources may no doubt yield much more information of the kind collected by Sabbe,[1] and the numismatical material is far from exhausted, nor is the true role of money satisfactorily explained. The cultural development has been the step-child of the discussion, and this field offers vast opportunities for research. It might prove important to ascertain if new trends of art, literature, or philosophy spread quickly from one region to another, and it would be valuable to examine what knowledge of Oriental affairs is displayed by European authorities, as Baynes and Iorga have done in some cases. This must then be supplemented by similar examinations of Oriental sources, for it must not be forgotten that an economic and cultural intercourse has always two sides; the Oriental side has definitely been grossly neglected, and many historians entirely lack knowledge of Oriental conditions. For this we must turn to specialists in Islamic and Byzantine history, and very likely they will get the last word.

But more than anything else a revision of the very formulation of the problems is needed. Much vagueness and many possibilities of conflict have been caused by the lack of clear definitions. This is true of the cultural history, since nobody takes the trouble to define precisely what they mean by a cultural unity, and within economic history many speak in vague general terms about natural and money economy without defining these conceptions. The greatest deficiency is, however, the lack of definitions of the Orient and the Occident. Most participants in the discussion seem to localize the Orient in the Levant proper and the Southern Balkans, while the Occident is identified with Italy and the Frankish kingdom. But though this may seem obvious, it is in fact a fatal bias, evoked by modern geographical notions. For the later Roman empire it should be natural to define the

Orient and the Occident as respectively the Eastern and the Western empire. But through Justinian's conquests the Orient took large parts of the Occident into possession, not only politically, but to a certain degree also culturally and economically. This means that the cultural, particularly the religious contrast before the 7th century, was not a contrast between the Orient and the Occident, but between two parties within the Orient. Greece had a considerable orthodox party, and the pope still regarded the Byzantine emperor as the true secular head of the world and dated all letters by the imperial years of reign until 787. Furthermore, most of the Balkans was subject to the ecclesiastical jurisdiction of Rome.

The Islamic expansion incorporated Africa and Spain into the Moslem Orient, and the Balkans and Sicily came under the Constantinopolitan patriarch during the iconoclastic conflict, while at the same time Byzantine Italy was truly hellenized. This development confined the Occident to the domain of the Roman church, and Western unity was further emphasized by Charlemagne's conquests, which brought all Roman Catholic countries, except the British Isles, together under one ruler. Thus in the age of Charlemagne the Occident stood out as a definite conception in contrast to the Orient, but at the same time it enjoyed an intimate contact with both the Moslem and the Byzantine Orient via respectively Spain and Italy, for wheresoever Allah was worshipped, or the Greek emperor obeyed, the Orient was present. Such a conception in the highest degree simplifies the problem of the economic and cultural relations between the Orient and the Occident, since the western parts of the Islamic and Byzantine Orient were never without connexion with the eastern parts.

Nothing is better proof of Pirenne's brilliant eloquence than the fact that he has been able to impose his own formulation of the problems upon even his opponents, but by now the time should be ripe for an unbiased revision.

---

[1] E. Sabbe, a Belgian historian, has brought to light considerable evidence of trade between East and West in the Carolingian period. [Editor's note]

An attempt to draft a list of supplementary references on the "Pirenne Thesis" encounters two fundamental difficulties. In the first place, so wide are the ramifications and so broad are the implications of Pirenne's ideas that a bibliography might well embrace the entire history of the Middle Ages. In the second place, the issues are of primary concern to European historians, more especially French, German, and Belgian, and most of their contributions (whether in book form or in articles) are not available in English translation and indeed may be consulted only in a few American libraries. A list of references for undergraduate use in the United States must, therefore, be necessarily arbitrary.

The purpose of the suggestions which follow is two-fold: (1) to suggest some introductory material which may be helpful to the beginning student and to provide him with a larger context for the analysis of this problem; (2) to indicate to the student where he will find further elaboration of the issues raised by Pirenne and more extensive criticism than is found in the selections provided in this booklet.

For the student, just beginning to find his way in the period, the problem can best be studied initially in conjunction with some standard survey of the early Middle Ages. If this survey is conventional in nature and moderate in interpretation, so much the better, for then the impact of Pirenne will be all the greater. There are many such surveys available in excellent texts. A very serviceable introduction in even briefer compass is found in Joseph R. Strayer, *Western Europe in the Middle Ages: A Short History* (New York, 1955).

The larger the context the student can provide for himself, the better. It would be well for him to become thoroughly acquainted with the political story of the barbarian invasions and the formation of Germanic kingdoms in the West. Analyses which are fairly comprehensive and yet within manageable compass are found in J. M. Wallace-Hadrill, *The Barbarian West, 400–1000* (London, 1952) and in H. St. L. B. Moss, *The Birth of the Middle Ages, 395–814* (London, 1935). An ambitious student will be rewarded by consulting the mass of information in the early volumes of the *Cambridge Medieval History*. Ferdinand Lot, much influenced by Pirenne, was the author of a brilliant treatment of the transition from the Roman Empire to Germanic kingdoms in his *The End of the Ancient World and the Beginnings of the Middle Ages* (New York, 1931).

The difficult problem of the relation of the Merovingian period to the Carolingian era may be pursued in several distinguished works. One of the most important of recent years is that of E. Salin, *La Civilisation mérovingienne d'après les sépultures, les textes et le laboratoire* (2 vols., Paris, 1950–1953). Salin, a French mining engineer turned archaeologist, has framed novel and significant theories concerning the Merovingian period. His first volume is a general treatment of the German invasions; the second is an analysis of grave findings. Easily the best work on the Carolingian era is Louis Halphen, *Charlemagne et l'empire carolingien* (Paris, 1947). The leading Austrian medievalist of the twentieth century has been the late Alfons Dopsch. He held to the notion of unbroken cultural and economic continuity from the later Roman Empire through the Merovingian period into the Carolingian era. His views have been accepted only in part and should be studied with caution; they may be followed in his *The Economic and Social Foundations of European Civilization* (condensed and translated from the second German edition; New York, 1937). Arthur Jean Kleinclausz, *Charlemagne* (Paris, 1934) is the best book in any language on its subject, but a very readable and dependable biography is available in Richard Winston's *Charlemagne, from the Hammer to the Cross* (New York, 1955).

Byzantine studies are now enjoying a renaissance and provide another vantage point from which to assess the ideas of Pirenne. A good introduction is offered in J. M. Hussey, *The Byzantine World* (London, 1957). A standard work is A. A. Vasiliev, *History of the Byzantine Empire* (2 vols., Madison, Wis., 1928–1929). Vasiliev was a Russian scholar who came to the United States in 1925 and was long associated with the University of Wisconsin and with the Dumbarton Oaks Research Library. His book was also published in Russian, French, Spanish, and Turkish. Less detailed but somewhat more abreast of latest scholarship is a work by the Serbian scholar, Georg Ostrogorsky. His *History of the Byzantine State* (Oxford, 1956) is a translation from the second German edition of 1954, but incorporates results of research even in the brief interim. An interesting presentation of the issues of Byzantine history is afforded by comparative study of the views of a French historian, Ch. Diehl (1859–1944) and those of a British scholar, Norman H. Baynes (1877–   ). A student seeking more general treatment, particularly of cultural history, will do well to consult the essays by specialists in various fields conveniently collected by Norman H. Baynes and H. St. L. B. Moss, in *Byzantium: An Introduction to East Roman Civilization* (Oxford, 1948). It is a valuable and fascinating book. A useful treatment of the same material, but more popular in tone, is provided in Steven Runciman, *Byzantine Civilisation* (London, 1933).

For Islam, the important contribution of Philip K. Hitti, an Arab scholar at Princeton since 1926, will provide ample material. His *The Arabs: A Short History* (Princeton, 1943) is a highly successful compression of a much larger work, *History of the Arabs* (5th edition, London, 1953). Gustav E. von Grunebaum in *Medieval Islam: A Study in Cultural Orientation* (2nd ed., Chicago, 1953) has much to say concerning Moslem ideas and institutions which is relevant to the controversy over Pirenne.

The most elusive problems raised by Pirenne are those which concern economic development — trade, industry, towns, and cities. Until very recently, in these matters the state of our knowledge made the early medieval period indeed a "dark age." Contemporary sources on economic history are far scantier than for political or for church history. Only a few documents before 800 are found in a recent collection of materials put together by Robert S. Lopez and Irving W. Raymond (*Medieval Trade in the Mediterranean World*, New York, 1955). But medieval economic history is now a very active field; the works already cited by Lot, Dopsch, Salin, and Halphen incorporate results of recent research. The most useful summaries in English, as well as extensive bibliographies, will be found in vol. I–II of the *Cambridge Economic History* (Cambridge, 1941, 1952). But the best book on economic development in the early Middle Ages is now Robert Latouche, *Les Origines de l'économie occidentale* (Paris, 1956).

The serious student interested in trends of current scholarship will soon become aware of the rich resources in scholarly periodicals concerned with the early Middle Ages; the journal most readily available to undergraduates will be *Speculum: A Journal of Medieval Studies,* published by the Medieval Academy of America. At the same time he will do well to become acquainted with the contributions of historians of other days. In this connection, Edward Gibbon's *History of the Decline and Fall of the Roman Empire* (Bury edition, 7 v., London, 1896–1900) is of course a work apart and should still be read both for its information and its interpretation.

For Henri Pirenne himself, the essentials for the examination of his ideas and the controversy they generated are found in the selections of this book. Further amplification and illustration can, however, readily be found. Professor Gray C. Boyce provides some interesting biographical details, including Pirenne's poignant experience during the first World War, in his article, "The Legacy of Henri Pirenne," *Byzantion*, vol. XV (1940–1941), pp. 449–464. A full reading of the *Mohammed and Charlemagne* will provide fairly complete knowledge of Pirenne's contribution. A comprehensive bibliography of Pirenne's writings is found in Henri Laurent, "Les Travaux de M. Henri Pirenne sur la fin du monde antique et les débuts du moyen âge," *Byzantion*, VII (1932), 495–509, and in Anne Riising, "The Fate of Henri Pirenne's Theses," *Classica et Mediaevalia*, XIII (1952). The more important items, with citations to reviews of Pirenne's books, are found in Daniel C. Dennett, Jr., "Pirenne and Muhammad," *Speculum*, XXIII (April, 1948). A careful defense of Pirenne is provided in Pierre Lambrechts, "Les Thèses de Henri Pirenne sur la fin du monde antique et les débuts du moyen âge," *Byzantion*, XIV (1939), 513–536. A recent analysis is that by Anne Riising (in the article cited above); she cites and summarizes the important commentary which has accumulated over the years.

DATE DUE